Operation Fly Trap

Operation Fly Trap

L.A. Gangs, Drugs, and the Law

SUSAN A. PHILLIPS

THE UNIVERSITY OF CHICAGO PRESS   CHICAGO AND LONDON

SUSAN A. PHILLIPS is professor of environmental analysis at Pitzer College and the author of
Wallbangin': Graffiti and Gangs in L.A.

The University of Chicago Press, Chicago 60637
The University of Chicago Press, Ltd., London
© 2012 by The University of Chicago
All rights reserved. Published 2012.
Printed in the United States of America

21 20 19 18 17 16 15 14 13 12   1 2 3 4 5

ISBN-13: 978-0-226-66765-2 (cloth)
ISBN-13: 978-0-226-66766-9 (paper)
ISBN-10: 0-226-66765-0 (cloth)
ISBN-10: 0-226-66766-9 (paper)

Library of Congress Cataloging-in-Publication Data

Phillips, Susan A., 1969–
    Operation Fly Trap : L.A. gangs, drugs, and the law / Susan A. Phillips.
        p. cm.
    Includes bibliographical references and index.
    ISBN-13: 978-0-226-66765-2 (alk. paper)
    ISBN-10: 0-226-66765-0 (alk. paper)
    ISBN-13: 978-0-226-66766-9 (pbk. : alk. paper)
    ISBN-10: 0-226-66766-9 (pbk. : alk. paper) 1. Gangs—California—Los Angeles—Case
studies. 2. Drug control—Social aspects—United States. 3. Drug traffic—Investigation—
California—Los Angeles—Case studies. 4. Gang prevention—California—Los Angeles—
Case studies. 5. Drug enforcement agents—California—Los Angeles—Case studies.
6. Informers—California—Los Angeles—Case studies. I. Title.
    HV6439.U7P465 2012
    363.4509794'94—dc23

                                                        2011036114

♾ This paper meets the requirements of ANSI/NISO Z39.48-1992 (Permanence of Paper).

FOR ALEX AND KATHERINE

Contents

Acknowledgments

Many people have helped shape this book. My work in the Pueblos would have been impossible without the friendship of Ben Kapone (now deceased), and without the love and acceptance of his family and friends, especially Nakisha Lee, Robert Johnson, Tracy Duffin, and Linda Clemmons (now deceased). In the Villains neighborhood, I thank Genia Jackson for opening her home to me and for putting me in contact with other Fly Trap family members. Much earlier, in 1995, I had been an intern at the Black Women's Health Project in that same neighborhood, and I thank Frances Jemmott and Eloise Joseph for launching me into the community work that would culminate in this project.

For early and sustained support of research and writing, I thank Tom Hayden, George Lipsitz, Barry Sanders, and Diego Vigil. For help with mapping, statistics, and crime data analysis, I thank Jeff Godown and Nathan Ong of the Los Angeles Police Department's (LAPD) COMPSTAT unit, Lee Munroe of Pitzer College, and Warren Roberts at Honnold-Mudd Library. I was able to interview two law enforcement leaders for this project. I am grateful to Los Angeles County Sheriff Lee Baca and District Attorney Steve Cooley, and to their respective offices. Sally Swartz at Federal Correctional Institution Dublin facilitated interviews inside that institution, and Susan McKee at the FBI guided me through formal permissions for interviews. I thank the FBI and LAPD media relations departments for granting approval for research. Marc Mauer of the Sentencing Project met with me early on to discuss federal sentencing law, and John Mutter of Columbia University's Earth Institute explained the impact of stress on women's lives post–Hurricane Katrina as I sought a frame of comparison for my project. Robert Weisberg at Stanford Law School and Nkechi Taifa at the Open Society Policy Center helped tighten the chapter on federal sentencing policy. I extend my gratitude to all of these people.

For writerly support, I am indebted to Rhoda Janzen and Peter Jurmu. Peter's sharp editorial eye transformed my writing into a far more respectable final product. Along the way, my transcribers were indispensible: Delores Abdella, Pati La Belle, and especially Emily Baird. The two babysitters who gave me time to work while being a mom were Letty and Jassel Roman. Friends Kirsten Olson and Rosemarie Ashamalla sustained me through the ups and downs of this project. Several family members became critical readers: Ralph Jungheim, Bob Klang, Silvia Milosevich, and Maria Phillips. The affection with which my entire family surrounded me for the duration of this work was heartwarming.

This project would not have been possible without the people directly involved in Operation Fly Trap who placed their trust in me. FBI special agent Robert King set a tone of openness early on, and my attempts to live up to his expectations have provided this project with much needed balance. LAPD detective Mark Brooks gave informative, insightful, and engaging accounts of his life as a cop, and of Operation Fly Trap in particular. This book would have been sorely lacking without these two individuals' willingness to share experiences, lessons, and opinions with me. Fly Trap targets Kevin Allen, John Edwards, Tawana Edwards, Tina Jackson, and Juan Lococo comprise the heart of this story, and their lives continue to be in open navigation. These individuals, and their family and friends—in particular Debbie Edwards, Brian Favors, Jorgina Gomez, Juanita Gomez, Ann Kennon, and Desiree Thomas—gave their stories because they believed I could represent their experiences for a broader audience. I count myself lucky to have expanded my circle of research, family, and friends to include them.

The Harry Frank Guggenheim Foundation awarded me the research grant that began this project in 2005, and in particular I would like to recognize HFG program director Karen Colvard. A Soros Justice Media Fellowship in 2008 allowed me to spend a year writing. Being part of the Soros network is a tremendous privilege, and Adam Culbreath and Christina Voight facilitated my entrance into it. Pitzer College supported this work through summer research funding and by granting me leave for fieldwork and writing.

I owe John Hagedorn and one anonymous reviewer a tremendous intellectual debt for the critical feedback that reshaped this text into a more rigorous and accessible document. I am also indebted to Kathryn Gohl for her meticulous copy editing of the manuscript. All flaws in this text are mine alone.

At the University of Chicago Press, I thank Priya Nelson and my editor, T. David Brent. David has been a staunch supporter and friend for many years. Working with him has been one of the great pleasures of my career.

My husband, Erik Blank, and my two children, Alex and Katherine, have always given me unquestioning support and love. I started this project the month before Alex, now eight, was born, and the book is reaching its conclusion as Katherine turns three. I could not function a day without them.

Introduction

CHARLOTTE VENIA JACKSON, a/k/a CHARLOTTE RENE JACKSON, CHARLETTE TINA JACKSON, CHAR-
LOTTE VENDA JACKSON, TINA JACKSON, NICJNEY HONES, CHALOTTE VENTRA JACKSON, RENADA
JOHNSON, CHARLOTTE VENA JACKSON, RICKNEY HONES, NICKEY JONES, RENADA CARLETTE
JOHNSON, RENADA C. JACKSON, RENADA CARLOTTE JOHNSON, RENADA CHARLOTTE JOHNSON,
CHARLOTTE VENIA JACKSON, NIGKNEY JOHNES and TINA FLY

When Tina Fly was eight years old, she put a firecracker in a class-mate's ear. Tina was a nearly illiterate child. The incessant teas-ing by other students compounded her behavioral problems, like the firecracker incident, and eventually she was put in special classes. Her mother, Genia Jackson, remembers a doctor prescribing Ritalin for Tina when she was nine, which was the beginning of years of trips to the physi-cian and psychologist. Tina attempted suicide at fourteen. She afterward cycled through mental hospitals and treatment centers throughout South Los Angeles and Watts. She was diagnosed alternately with bipolar disor-der, schizophrenia, depression, and, much later, "borderline mental retar-dation." She claimed she sometimes heard the voice of her father telling her to kill herself, or, contrarily, to "be strong." She was a lesbian lover of Linda Bayer, a Fly Trap target dubbed Black, and Crystal, a half-black, half-Mexican crack addict who eventually became Confidential Source 1.

Tina met John Edwards, or "Junior," at sixteen and shortly thereafter became pregnant with Tawana, the eldest of her two daughters. Junior was her first real romance and remains the man she describes as the love of her life. In adulthood, they became "crimies"—partners in crime—but as teens they were embroiled in attraction and dependence. Before Fly Trap, Junior's only violent criminal charge was related to domestic vio-lence against Tina. When he found out that Tina had lied by telling him he was the father of her next child, Joanna, however, he didn't care. He continued to provide care for the girl, another challenged child, who, with her grandmother's help, eventually graduated from high school.

Every time Tina was incarcerated, authorities medicated her. At twenty, she began the crack abuse that would last for the next two decades. No trauma or life-changing event drove her to addiction: when a friend gave her the first hit, she wanted more. In the mid-1990s, Tina became a prostitute to support her habit. She did demoralizing things on crack, she says, that she never would have done otherwise. She left her kids with her mother and ran wild on Central Avenue.

When the FBI arrested and charged Tina in 2003, she had no technical grounds on which to base an insanity plea, but the court psychologist recommended that the judge take her poor impulse control and susceptibility to manipulation into account during sentencing. She had, however, been caught on wiretap planning to exploit her mental health history by acting unstable. She boasted of paying a mental health worker to testify for her. In court, she argued that she had worked for Junior in fear, that Kevin Allen, or "K-Rok," was her pimp, and that she had been dealing drugs to support her drug habit. But the wiretap showed that, despite her disabilities, Tina Fly ran things and ran people, so much so that the FBI had named the entire task force after her: Operation Fly Trap.

Operation Fly Trap began in 2001 at a picnic table behind LAPD's Newton Division station on Central Avenue during a conversation between Officer Mark Brooks of the LAPD and Special Agent Robert King of the FBI. Special Agent King was in L.A. on another case, and the two had previously met during the takedown of 38th Street, the historic Latino gang neighborhood of Sleepy Lagoon fame. Brooks proposed that he and King work together against gangs in two nearby Bloods neighborhoods, the Pueblo Bishops and the Blood Stone Villains. Gunfire intended for a gang member had recently killed an innocent woman on her porch; Brooks's lieutenant was pressuring area officers for results. The LAPD applied this pressure whenever violence ramped up in the neighborhoods around Newton Division.

Brooks had been around a long time and knew everyone in the neighborhoods he patrolled. He had watched the kids grow into gang members of the most lethal kind: violent and on drugs, uneducated, and lacking empathy. He had started his own childhood in a similar neighborhood, but his mother had moved from Watts and Compton to Texas. There, he had chosen a different path, and made it, something he liked to remind the young g's of when he encountered them on the street. He knew, he says, that the neighborhood was full of good people, but it was his job to get the others, like these gang members, who spread poison in the community. Brooks and King began to lay the groundwork for a new task force to draw out that poison permanently, if possible.

The Pueblo Bishops and Blood Stone Villains, two adjacent African American Bloods neighborhoods, hold down the 50s blocks between Central Avenue and Alameda Street in Los Angeles. The relationship between Pueblos and Villains is often contentious, but historically they had been close allies who never engaged in a full-scale gang war. Rumors abounded that members of the other gang had AIDS, and there were squabbles over all kinds of neighborhood issues. Thirty years of love, friendship, partying, and rivalry came out in all kinds of crazy ways that didn't necessarily lead to lethal violence. The two allied gangs used to write their names together: PBSV for Pueblo Bishops–Blood Stone Villains. By 2000, however, tensions between the two neighborhoods had increased. Pressure from nearby Crip gangs had kept the two Bloods neighborhoods united, but the gradual dissolution of the Blood–Crip ideological rivalry beginning in 1992, and the demographic shift from Black to Latino in the area, sparked chronic fighting within the two gangs as well as with 38th Street, a Latino gang just to the north of them. The Operation Fly Trap task force intended to stop this warfare by targeting the area's lucrative underground drug economy and its key players.

Genia Jackson watched it all happen from a distance. "*That* ride," she said later. "I'll never forget *that* ride," from the morning officers had burst into her house to the day in court when she heard the wiretap recordings of her daughter's voice talking about drugs and fake paperwork. Over the year following the arrest, Ms. Jackson dropped ten pounds from her already slender frame and had to be hospitalized. Her other daughter began suffering from chronic headaches for which she also required hospitalization. To make things worse, Tina's two-year-old grandson had internalized the motions of raised hands and spread-eagled legs and would respond automatically to cues for secure entrance into the federal Metropolitan Detention Center in downtown Los Angeles where Tina was being held. That broke her heart most, Ms. Jackson said. At two years old, that little boy already knew how to go to jail.

Genia Jackson had lived on 56th Street for thirty years. She remembered when the first Mexican family had moved into the neighborhood; her own black family was now one of the last on the block. Ms. Jackson was known to her neighbors as a "firm person." She frequently called the police on kids in the neighborhood, and she opened her garage to the kids when they had problems to discuss. She worked hard for her church and organized women's day events and worship activities. She had been a block captain and was devastated by Officer Brooks's targeting of her family: "Why mines?" she demanded. "Why not these?" she asked, pointing to the cadre of girls on the corner who continued to deal drugs after the task force. She had until then been so proud of Tina, knowing that Tina was finally living on her own, that she had cleaned herself up from her addictions, that she was no longer running the streets, that she was paying her own rent and managing her own household.

The drug game, however, was what had inspired Tina to get clean and had kept her afloat. It was her new addiction, she said: fast money. Neither the most powerful nor the least, Tina was at the center of everything. She was the one always calling, the one always coming or going. She connected everyone, from the highest to the lowest. She was everywhere, all the time.

Painstakingly, Brooks and King built their case. They recruited confidential sources. They stationed themselves in undercover vehicles and made strategic arrests. But their informants were too scared to give good information, and their undercover cars were always identified. After the task force won the right to wiretap cell phone communications, all this became moot. Brooks and King now knew everything about everybody: who was dating whom, who was fighting, and who was selling, and for how much. The drug verbiage of chickens, birds, bricks, cookies, ones, twos, and fives became the language of their everyday world. Within a two-year period, they had successfully uncovered the network. They assembled a list of twenty-eight names, obtained warrants, and gathered the resources of over thirty collaborating law enforcement agencies. Then, at dawn on June 26, 2003, they started breaking down doors.

* * *

November 1, 2007, was a day of celebration in federal penitentiaries throughout the United States. Congress had chosen not to challenge the U.S. Sentencing Commission's recommendation to reduce penalties for crack cocaine. This victory was the first of two in a twenty-year battle that activists, organizers, families, and the Sentencing Commission itself had been fighting to overturn what many regarded as the most racist piece of active legislation in the United States. The Anti-Drug Abuse Act of 1986 had required that the amount of powder cocaine needed to trigger a mandatory minimum sentence was a hundred times the amount of crack necessary for such a trigger. Numbers were clear. Eighty percent of those convicted under crack laws were African American. The congressional inaction on November 1 didn't directly address the 100:1 disparity, but it did allow judges more leeway in sentencing people on the basis of prior criminal history. Several Fly Trap targets were among 19,000 prisoners now eligible to shave an average of sixteen months off their sentences.

President Obama's election in 2008 brought an even greater victory. On August 3, 2010, Obama signed the Fair Sentencing Act into law, reducing the crack/cocaine disparity to 18:1. Optimism and anxiety now weighted the lives of already convicted individuals, who awaited news of whether the legal change would eventually apply to them.

Although Operation Fly Trap predated these legislative changes, it was part of the same sociolegal moment. The public had de facto withdrawn support for the drug war. Political battle cries to be tough on crime now stopped short of proposing long sentences for nonviolent offenders. The Federal Bureau of Prisons—now the largest single prison system in the United States—was vulnerable to a critique that 90 percent of its inmates were nonviolent.[1] Operation Fly Trap was part of an attempt to make this 90 percent more palatable by recasting nonviolent drug offenders as intimately related to the lethal violence of gangs.

Diane Feinstein, Democratic senator from California, had long supported rectifying the racialized sentencing disparities in the federal system. But Feinstein also hated the gangs that posed a significant problem in her home state. In 2007, and again in 2009, federal antigang legislation she had spent years crafting was finally to go before Congress. The Gang Prevention and Abatement Act expanded the list of gang crimes that could be penalized within the federal system. Opponents said the law was costly and unnecessary. Federal gang prosecutions were already possible through RICO, gun laws, and other conspiracy-based charges. Proponents of the act said that we needed more. They argued that gangs devastated communities and had been in part responsible for a nationwide rise in violent crime. Had the act passed, it would have become the most significant new contributor to racial disparities within the federal system, now masked by a veneer of gang violence.[2]

Operation Fly Trap was just one point of connection between drugs and gangs in a time of criminal policy crisis and adjustment. Sentencing reforms, the Feinstein legislation, and task forces like Fly Trap all answered a need to re-present the drug war as healthy and justifiable.

Testimony by Debra Yang, Central Division's U.S. attorney, made much the same point. Before the U.S. Senate Committee on the Judiciary, Yang lauded the Fly Trap case among others her office had prosecuted, indicating that "members of these gangs had terrorized their respective communities, such as the Pueblo Del Rio housing project in Los Angeles, for years with a vice-like grip on the drug trade in their communities. The gang members backed up that iron grip with the ever present shadow of violence, both real and threatened."[3]

Despite brief national attention, little about Fly Trap was remarkable. It was no Tulia, where one crooked cop left 20 percent of black men in that Texas town incarcerated erroneously.[4] It didn't exemplify the worst abuses in policing, as had, for example, the LAPD Rampart Division scandals beginning in the late 1990s. Nor did Fly Trap involve the purportedly worst kinds of criminals. By 2003, that spot had been reserved for members of Mara Salvatrucha, a transnational gang with ties to Latin America. Operation Fly Trap was one of roughly 250 similar task forces mounted nationwide in 2003, and the best it had to offer were some run-of-the-mill Bloods, a couple of significant drug dealers, one bona fide supplier, and a high conviction rate.

For me, Fly Trap's daily aspect was more valuable than a splashy corruption story or a series of handpicked anecdotes. Commonplace police work reveals more detail about how law enforcement and legal proceedings define relations of power. The manner in which power is written through law is a daily thing, after all, and requires unpacking daily stories, daily relationships, daily language.

Between criminal and law enforcement worlds, the ethnography of the individual relationships in Fly Trap feeds into an analysis of culturally constructed aspects of crime. Teasing apart connections among gangs, drugs, and policing in the context of drug policy failure adds to our understanding of penality's impact in segregated urban areas, the relationship of gang violence to a state restructuring itself around security issues, and the widespread use of criminal justice methods to address social problems.

Operation Fly Trap's rhetoric tended to boil down gang violence to a single cause: the drug trade. But gangs are far more complicated. None of the major drug dealers in the case was an active gang member, though all lived in gang neighborhoods. The rivalry the task force intended to disrupt had its roots outside of drug concerns. The police indicated that, for them, drugs were a convenient way to target those they considered to be key players.

As a global industry, the drug trade reinforces hierarchy at the same time as it provides a great economic equalizer. Most illegal drugs are manufactured outside of the United States but consumed within its borders, making U.S. drug consumption a prime mover in an industry the U.N. estimates is worth $320 billion dollars annually. Illicit drugs now comprise 0.9 percent of the global Gross Domestic Product, a trade that bolsters crumbling local economies from Bolivia to Baltimore.[5]

As in other North American cities, "serving" or "slangin'" in Los Angeles forms a bridge over defunct union manufacturing jobs and service-sector employment made inaccessible by public school failure.[6] With these barren economic circumstances, the drug game has become a powerful opportunity rooted in local neighborhoods, which in Los Angeles are ruled almost exclusively by gangs.

In L.A., long-term familial involvement in the drug trade follows patterns of economic deindustrialization. The hiring practices of the 1970s, when the key Fly Trap targets were children, exhibited the same overt racism toward black men as they had in the 1940s and 1950s. The oil crisis had begun; the dollar was depreciating in the international market. In 1973, union jobs had begun shrinking in L.A. During the rest of the decade, the bifurcation of the manufacturing sector would take its toll on L.A.'s working class, as it did in many American cities. The education system simply failed to keep up with these changes. Between 1970 and 2003, California public schools went from best to worst. Many who might otherwise have held factory jobs instead became part of a generation of drug dealers, drug users, and gang members. In the 1970s states still competed for the lowest number of prisoners. In those days, low numbers of incarcerated individuals meant a healthy society, not the other way around.[7]

Geographer Ruth Gilmore writes of the multiple surpluses that turned this low-incarceration equation on its head.[8] Californians had grown tired of using their money to build the state's infrastructure. The taxpayer revolt of the mid-1970s disinvested many from the public school system and other public works projects, leaving the role of state government in question. Drought simultaneously left land fallow in rural parts of the state, and an entire generation of would-be working-class people had no employment. These surpluses created a perfect storm in which building a massive prison infrastructure, though not inevitable, became California's salvation enterprise. From 1973 to 2003, the state's prison system increased from twelve to forty institutions—the fastest rate of growth "anyone, anywhere has ever seen," says prison researcher Elliot Currie.[9] Incarceration became California's number one industry. It would grow to employ the largest number of people in the state and would eventually boast the most powerful union, the California Correctional Peace Officers Association—prison guards.

This California trend continues to echo at the federal level. The federal prison population has increased by more than 500 percent in the past twenty-five years and remains on an upward trajectory. The Federal Bureau of Prisons (FBOP) went from housing 21,539 inmates in 1979 to 217,444 in 2011, and 75 percent of those sentenced in the federal system are people of color. Although the California prison system has now hit stasis, the FBOP continues to expand with the increasing federalization of crime—so much so that the feds have begun to use private prisons to take up the slack.[10]

Most of this rampant prison growth is attributable to the war on drugs. In the wake of deindustrialization, it became possible to wage a war that targeted drug use and sales. Jailing such a significant portion of the working class never could have happened if those same individuals had been needed in the labor force, even if they had been using or dealing drugs.[11] At the federal level, mandatory minimum sentencing and other policy changes began to flood the system with drug offenders and kept them there longer. Drug offenders are now 55 percent of the FBOP population.[12]

Although intended to solve problems of crime and violence, crime suppression—and particularly incarceration—has resulted in many of the same disruptions for families as has massive job loss. Incarceration has become as significant a multigenerational process as the deindustrialized economy that preceded it and that continues in its wake. Consistently targeted communities with deep local ties are simply unable to transform incarceration or reentry into anything positive at collective or individual levels.[13] Fly Trap, in its turn, incarcerated a group of individuals intimately related to one another through kinship and neighborhood affiliation. Although a precise attack, it impacted the lives of far more people than the targeted individuals.

I began to follow the fallout of Operation Fly Trap among several families soon after the June takedown. Violence was difficult to gauge in the two neighborhoods, and the families of those arrested were dealing with court dates, financial instability, health problems, child social services, job loss, and eviction proceedings. The wife of one Fly Trap target lost her job and was denied unemployment benefits. She and her two children remained without income or health insurance for eight months. The mother of another target described having her apartment raided three times: once for the target (who was apprehended), once for another son who was and had been in prison for the past five years, and once for a son who was deceased. Neighborhood residents freely bandied about the identities of the confidential informants who had ratted them out. One Fly Trap court case proved that sheriff's deputies had falsified paperwork regarding hard evidence in order to match the date of his recorded conversation with a source.

By the time of Fly Trap and its attendant stories, I had spent a great deal of time in the Pueblos and Villains neighborhoods. Beginning in 1995, I had volunteered for a year at the Black Women's Health Project in the heart of the Villains' neighborhood, educating myself about women's health, about Bloods, Crips, and Latino gangs, and about the significance of the 1992 rioting. For the next ten years, vague thoughts of ethnography shaped my time in the neighborhoods, and I developed a close relationship with one particular family in the Pueblos. Ben Kapone, a subsequent Fly Trap target from the Pueblo Bishops, had early on taken me under his wing after we met in the projects. His five-year-old brother and eighteen-year-old sister became the strongest connections between us.

In the years that followed, Ben's name offered me protection despite the fact that he was incarcerated most of the time I knew him. When he was inside, I grew close to his family, his mother, wife, sisters, younger brother, and his children, nieces and nephews, aunts and uncles. I experienced many of the family's joys and difficulties, facing along with them the death of Ben's five-year-old nephew who was hit by a car, the loss of his three-month-old grandbaby accidentally smothered by a grandmother's epileptic seizure, and the loss of a twenty-five-year-old nephew dead from swallowing drugs as he fled police. Joys were often not far off these tragedies. The kids would make peashooters in the summertime, capture sand bees in plastic water bottles, and jump on me whenever I walked in the door. At times, the Pueblos gang had been at its strongest, with members visible and in the streets. Most of them were so suspicious of me that my time in the neighborhood was frankly painful. Ben's protection never equaled acceptance. Other times, the gang was weaker, with people of importance inside or dead.

When Ben became a Fly Trap target, Ben's family crumbled. The notion of family dissolution shaped the beginnings of a formal research project and part of this book's outcome.

Fly Trap jailed Ben at a time when he was attempting to go straight, not for the first time. He had held a legitimate job from January to June

2003, was being considered for early release from parole, and he and his wife were considering a move to Atlanta to cement his positive direction. But a Fly Trap surveillance unit had recorded a drug transaction between Ben and a confidential informant six months earlier, and the subsequent state case landed Ben in prison for three years. A cocaine addiction tarnished the period after his release, and Ben alienated many people in the neighborhood as a result of it. He was murdered in the projects one early morning in March 2008. Ben left behind his wife and their young daughter, three sons (one of whom was his wife's child), as well as his brother, three sisters, and many nieces and nephews. His mother hung on through multiple strokes and chronic illness. She died a year after Ben did.

Ben was killed the same week that Fly Trap cocaine supplier Juan Lococo won his appeal. In Lococo's case, as in Tina's and Junior's, the amount of powder cocaine had been mathematically converted into crack quantities for the purposes of maximizing his sentence. The U.S. attorneys argued that the defendants' foreknowledge that the powder they sold would be eventually converted to crack justified the multiplication, which allowed a lengthier sentence. (I go into detail regarding this practice in chap. 5.) Lococo's appeal, which was published in the Ninth Circuit in 2008, was partially dismissed, affirmed, vacated, and remanded. The affirmation of the ruling involving wiretap got national attention. The less-publicized courtroom crack conversion was remanded. As a result of Lococo's repeated assertions that he had no knowledge that his powder would be turned to crack, the judge reduced Lococo's sentence from twenty-two to fourteen years. Lococo says now, "one thing the government counted on in this case was the ignorance of the people they arrested. They thought we were nothing but one dumb Mexican and a bunch of dumb black gang members."

When I asked Tina and Tawana what they would put into a book they were writing about themselves, they said simultaneously "everything." "The good and the bad," Tawana said. Tina simply stated, "the truth." John Edwards similarly told me, "if you continue to write truth in your book, God will bless you." At first, these responses differed from law enforcement's continual worry that I'd paint them in a bad light. They wondered if I would treat them fairly, if my work could compromise the appeals process, or if I might repeat negative stereotypes that vilified cops. Such worries in part caused the U.S. Attorney's Office to withhold interview approval with law enforcement until all targets were out of appeals, nearly cementing the one-sided story they feared. I did speak to Mark Brooks and talked to Special Agent King about his early life before the U.S. Attorney's Office finally approved formal interviews.

Although all of the interviews provided balance, this book was never intended to tell the entire Fly Trap story. Brooks and King, for example, were the de-facto directors of the task force, but they worked closely with a team of individuals I did not interview. "It took a ton of people to make this happen," King says. "Jose and Alex bled as much as we did." The same was true of the twenty-eight Fly Trap targets. Though I attempted to contact all of them, a core group self-selected, and it ultimately included the five or so individuals and their families at the center of the case. Unpacking just their stories proved a significant undertaking.

The research began simply. An FBI press release included a list of targets' names, and I obtained inmates' address information from the website of the Bureau of Prisons. The federal courthouse on Spring Street was my second home for a while, as I reviewed and copied legal files related to the case. I wrote letters to the targets that included a survey regarding the impact of their incarceration on their families, and I asked permission to contact outside family members. Prison phone calls, letters, and e-mails came in as I developed relationships with prisoners and their families.

Courtroom documents, interviews, and discussions with family members, prisoners, and law enforcement personnel enabled me to develop a broader vision for the project. Seeing Fly Trap solely as a story of family dissolution proved too one-sided. Instead, a more holistic accounting of Fly Trap touched on many people's lives and on key issues in criminal and social justice. The rhythm of research carried me from personal narratives to local contexts, from communal relationships to public policies, from specific encounters to global trends. This rhythm helped me set two goals early on. First was to use the story's sensational aspects to counter potentially exoticized outcomes. I wanted to temper images of would-be urban exotics with humanizing, contextualized portraits that would allow people to cross social boundaries instead of simply re-entrenching them. My second goal was to emphasize points often missing from popular treatment of crime by drawing attention to the social contexts that give rise to crime and by analyzing the unintended consequences of crime's suppression. Emphasizing what comes before and after crime—within and between moments of publicity—helps make the point that we need to pay as much attention to flaws in systems as we do to flaws in people. This manner of looking makes Fly Trap not just a story about a group of people, but also about the broader features, and failures, of social policy and law.

The Fly Trap case begs the question of how to write a story that casts no one as hero and no one as villain, where action and judgment are more about power and environment than right and wrong. Gangs and drugs are critical symbols in this story, sensationalist categories that can either side-step or head full steam into foundational issues at the root of gangs, incarceration, and inequality.

Globally, gang members work through honor complexes, engage in violent and criminal behaviors to establish social order, and use symbols to express collective identity. Gangs in the United States straddle a continuum between youth groups and criminal corporations. Since the 1940s, Los Angeles gangs have had intense relationships with law enforcement. Several wars on gangs have punctuated the twentieth century, including the current one that began in the late 1980s.[14] Today's multiagency sweeps are just one among a cluster of tactics designed to combat gangs.[15] Gang injunctions, enhancements, and specialized police units are all efforts to deal with gangs through a multifaceted strategy of suppression.[16]

The critique that gang sweeps randomly target every kid on the street in baggy pants is no longer valid in Los Angeles. Today's sweeps are diamond cut compared to the rough enterprises of the early 1990s, projects that might net just five convictions out of 2,000 weekend arrests.[17] The papers still call them "sweeps," but "task force" is the preferred moniker among insiders. Task force members approach their jobs with precision and justification. Though task forces are not infallible, their charges tend to stick.

A growing part of this precision has been law enforcement's ability to mount long-term, collaborative investigations between federal and local agencies. In L.A., the potential for federal involvement was never that far off: Los Angeles had housed an FBI field office since 1914. Pachuco gangs of the 1940s with purported links to Mexican fifth-column anarchists, as opposed to the Mafia of the East Coast, attracted early FBI attention.[18] In the decades that followed, crime and political unrest, particularly within communities of color, shaped new federal directions, which were bolstered by Richard Nixon's declaration of the first war on drugs in 1971.

The FBI's announcement of its Violent Crime Safe Streets Initiative in 1992 made gangs a national priority. Gangs had now spread from urban centers across the country. The L.A. riots had created a sense of urgency to halt gangs from targeting or moving into suburbs. By 2011, the FBI boasted 168 Safe Streets task forces across the United States, involving fifty-five FBI field offices.[19] Interjurisdictional policing in Los Angeles, a city now touted as the gang capital of the world, became a routine rather than exceptional practice.

Operation Fly Trap was one of over 5,000 gang investigations mounted nationally between 2001 and 2010. These have resulted in more than 57,000 arrests and 23,000 convictions. As with all of these cases, Fly Trap represented an increasingly common task force style. Likened to the mob busts of the 1920s, Fly Trap relied heavily on surveillance, undercover officers, and confidential informants, who gathered information about key players and helped to build the cases against them. According to the FBI's press release, "These tools and strong partnerships among law enforcement agencies at all levels have contributed to the successful penetration and dismantlement of violent criminal enterprises that plague the neighborhoods of Los Angeles."[20] The key Fly Trap targets, they said, were also wanted for other violent crimes, such as assault or murder. They reasoned that gang members had escaped prosecution because of their strategy of fear and intimidation. Such difficulties enabled officers to argue for the use of wiretaps, confidential informants, and other methods of surveillance, as well as to develop a collaboration involving roughly thirty government agencies.

After his appointment as Los Angeles' new police chief in 2002, former New Yorker Bill Bratton said: "This is basically my Rubicon, my opportunity once and for all to make the case that a philosophy I have helped champion—that I am famous for espousing—works."[21] Bratton was referring to broken windows theory, a policing strategy that targets low-level crime to net bigger criminals. Though it's been boiled down to a few simplistic examples, broken windows theory is a fairly sophisticated look at how neighborhoods work, what material conditions make people fearful, what calms their fears, and what policing has to do with it. Although the evidence supporting broken windows theory is debated, it has been adopted as a policing strategy across the United States.[22]

In Los Angeles, Bratton wanted to attack gangs like he had attacked Mafia in New York. But the new chief was confronted with neither classic crime families nor the nineteen or so squeegee men who had been declared Manhattan's number one nuisance. Instead, there were somewhere between 40,000 and 60,000 gang members in about 400 gangs whose shape was decidedly decentralized.

As a multiagency investigation, Fly Trap was not a stereotypical example of broken windows policing. But this and other task forces took to heart Bratton's ramped up L.A. motto: "Bust a drug dealer and you may catch a killer."[23] L.A.'s gangland was so entrenched that drug dealing—usually considered a major crime compared to littering or writing graffiti—was treated as the broken window that led to more serious violent crimes.[24]

After the Fly Trap takedown, authorities stated unequivocally that the sweep had penetrated and dismantled violent gangs. On the ground, perceptions of task force results were less certain. Some residents indicated that things had gotten "quieter," while others described the area as "still crazy." A few months after Fly Trap, for example, a fifteen-year-old boy was killed while his sister played basketball at Slauson Park, adjacent to Pueblo del Rio.

The fifteen-year-old was just one victim in a forty-year gang war that, by 2003, had already claimed 15,000 lives.[25] Feuding between Bloods and Crips in Los Angeles began during the childhoods of several Fly Trap targets. In 1969, Crips emerged after a period of calm following the 1965 Watts riots, and partly as a result of governmental disruption of black nationalist movements. Soon after, non-Crip gangs consolidated to form the Bloods, which included Brims and Pirus, and the two collectivities began chronic warfare. Later, Crips' remarkable numbers allowed infighting among Crip gangs as well as with Bloods. Bloods, by contrast, remained unified until internal conflicts, and warfare between black and Latino gangs, began in the late 1990s.

From an anthropological perspective, the shape of gang warfare mirrors nonstate models of conflict within and outside of nation-states. Divisive violence within groups peripheral to state systems is a common pattern, where chronic internal violence results from colonial or imperialist tactics, changing ecological or technological circumstances, or fluctuating state policies.[26] Although gangs lack an explicit agenda of political violence, their daily practice inhabits a space in which violence determines social order. Violence for gangs may be self-injurious, but it is also group defining.

Within broader contexts of disorder, violent groups easily become targets for punitive state-building projects.[27] These projects share a blurring of formerly distinct social boundaries, in which center and periphery, first world and third world, prison and ghetto, good guy and bad guy, or peace and conflict, may all be considered part of the same trajectory. In the United States, carceral projects have in part legitimated "the state policy of urban abandonment and punitive containment responsible for the parlous state of the contemporary ghetto."[28]

Multiple contextual factors inform the integration of gang networks with family and neighborhood life. Diego Vigil writes of "grim material conditions ... reproduced intergenerationally" that provide the foundation for gang integration into families and communities.[29] Sudhir Venkatesh argues that gangs play a dual community role because they are tied into a viable economy. He details the many benefits gangs provide, including protection to residents, but he also recognizes how gangs foment violence and draw police attention, both of which engender great suffering. John Hagedorn comes to parallel conclusions through an in-depth historical treatment of gangs in Chicago, ultimately deriding the field of criminology for being too aligned with law enforcement projects to be useful.[30]

In this research, I frequently approached Fly Trap's analysis through themes of opposition and duality. These enabled me to locate the basis of cultural misunderstanding, to discover how individuals played into larger social structures, and to identify potential areas of social change. By pairing concepts such as precision and disorder, voicelessness and victimhood, or discipline and control, I intended to lay claim to opposing concepts simultaneously rather than viewing them as mutually exclusive.

Tina's dualities, for example, were within herself. Who was she, really? Was she good or bad, truly ill or just manipulative? Her father's voice told her both to kill herself and to stay strong. When I met with her in person at FCI Dublin, I could tell she was uneducated, but her gaze challenged. For me, Tina's many ambiguities became symbolic of the entire Fly Trap project.

I also often considered the duality between cop Mark Brooks and target Kevin Allen, two black men who had gone in divergent directions. Could these men, if viewed as archetypes, survive one without the other? At stake in the research, through investigation into people and systems, was the construction of social life as a whole, which labored through resilience and vulnerability, community rupture and coalition, and the meaning of safety or justice. Sentences can be tolerated; snitches can be reabsorbed. Both violence and the lack of violence are indexes of social order. Whether people experience violence as victim or perpetrator, it bonds them in life-changing ways and becomes a counterforce to the state's own violent actions.

The conversations within this book define justice as a place where expectation and reality meet and either line up admirably or miss one another completely. Special Agent Rob King's wife, Lea Ann, for example, wanted to know why people who had the chance to turn their lives around would continually blow it. Ben Kapone, who had struggled with this problem most of his life, could have explained it to her. Kevin Allen wanted to know how Officer Brooks could contribute to a system that was basically

in the business of incarcerating people of his own race. Brooks in turn crit-
icized Allen and the rest of the targets for spreading poison in that self-
same community. Tawana Edwards chided the police for not "understanding people," while police accused persons like her of destroying families.
Imagining these folks in conversation with one another was symbolic for
me of the dialogues necessary to create social policy informed by communication and understanding rather than segregation and misinformation.

Officer Brooks once told me that gang members don't care about the
community. They rat each other out and fail to warn others of impending
enemy attack. Although this may sometimes be true, Brooks has worked
with gangs long enough to know that gang members do care about the
community. They care in ways that no one else can. The fact of the matter is that gang members have something that we do not. They have the
collective, which makes them enviable in a certain way. Recall philoso-
pher Alexis de Tocqueville's hypothesis that in the collective—in same-
ness—resides the truest form of human happiness.[31] But the collective
also makes gangs deplorable, directly opposed to the ethos of individual-
ism at the heart of the American tradition.

America's penchant for punishment sets us apart globally: we now incarcerate one in every hundred individuals.[32] That rates of incarceration
have little to do with rates of crime is a little-known social travesty. Incarceration rates largely have to do with changes in policy, and such changes
tend to stem from things other than crime trends.[33] Legislative changes
that build prison populations bear the undue influence of political lobbies,
corporate interests, and mass media. Private prison corporations cowrote
and sponsored Arizona's anti-immigrant SB-1070 in 2010. Publicity surrounding the death of Polly Klass led to the passage of the three strikes
law in 1994. The 1988 shooting death of UCLA student Karen Toshima by
Crips birthed the current war on gangs. Federal drug laws—the infamous
100:1—came to fruition in a similar manner, with the cocaine-related
death of basketball star Len Bias in 1986.[34]

Eighties crack was a bleak form of cocaine. It seemed to be produc-
ing extreme amounts of violence and heightened addiction, particularly
within the black community. Authorities would later recognize the crack
laws to be the result of a groundless moral panic, but it took twenty-five
years for this recognition to change the policies erected so hastily in its
wake. Ben remembered the drug's effect on the neighborhood:

> [Cocaine] was so motherfucking pure and so cold when it hit the neighbor-
> hood. When it hit the black neighborhood, the ghetto, it blew our fucking mind.

Cocaine? This shit make you feel this way? Snortin' it, then it went to primos, then it went to pipe. You go downtown, majority of the mufuckers that's downtown is blacks, fucked up, sleeping in boxes. Over what? Crack that fucked they family up, fucked they life up. It's a cold fuckin' addiction. I know people saying, ain't nobody told you to put that in your mouth. Ain't nobody made you smoke cocaine. Whatever chemicals is in the muthafuckas, they killin' us. They killing black folks down here.

Unlike Ben, who came to it late, Tina was hooked into crack early enough and long enough to reshape her existing difficulties. Self-medication with illicit drugs is just one example of the "baffling interface between the criminal justice system and the mental health system."[35] The systematic withdrawal of supportive state institutions has made incarceration a cure-all for failures in education, housing, addiction, unemployment, and mental illness alike.

Families, and not just apprehended criminals, feel the effects of police work most strongly. Although the main goal of these systems is to protect society, the suppression of crime can severely damage families and communities, the social units that have the best ability to prevent crime in the first place. For Fly Trap family members, every independent factor—such as a mom getting off drugs and getting her kids back—became part of the sweep for them, and the sweep became part of the ongoing struggle to survive lives already in crisis.

Places that suffer with poverty and endemic internalized violence often have local histories in which state surveillance has begun to replace informal, and potentially more successful, networks of control. In these worlds, notions of "informing" or "telling" or "watching" become tactics that divide working-class peoples. So-called snitches have become critical social symbols in places where surveillance is about tracking conspiracy and collectivity as opposed to disrupting individual behavior.[36] In places that harbor crime-paranoia complexes, social control through looking does not necessarily translate into self-control, if one defines that as the control of either crime or violence. Social control for both gang and law enforcement is equivalent to the control of information—a project that, for gangs, ranges from spatial circumvention to coercive violence.

Gary T. Marx asserts in *Undercover: Police Surveillance in America* that an equal number of morally corrupt individuals exist at every level of society. If given the opportunity, Marx demonstrates, middle-class people frequently deviate from a straight and narrow path and onto a criminal one. Their transgressions, however, rarely draw the punitive response that street crime does. Chronically watching and penalizing low-income street criminals constitutes a policy choice that cements social inequality within urban neighborhoods and in our broader society.[37] Understanding how inequality persists despite a shared desire for a more just world belies assumptions about the nature of democracy and its associated freedoms.

Juan Lococo's sister Gracie once told me that she believed people who become drug dealers have grown up "limited." They don't have what they should, and they crave, for the rest of the lives, something to fill holes in themselves—not enough food, no tennis shoes, no having what other kids have. One L.A. County sheriff described much the same problem, only he also cited broader social disengagement as a contributing factor:

> All the love that you don't get, you just kind of learn to live without it. I know that you can get through that if you want to. Take the path of least resistance at the time. But for most of the public, it's out of sight, out of mind. As an officer, you see the bodies laying around, you can smell the blood, then you go outside and see the kids not dressed right, without the right clothes on. If our society doesn't have to see this, or deal with it, they don't care about it.

According to Tom Hayden, over 25,000 mostly young people of color have died on L.A. streets as a result of gang wars. He writes, "these dead simply don't count. . . . The limited interpretation . . . is that death is deserved, that it stems from personal pathology."[38] Because the process of othering informs what people know about life or death in the ghetto, moral views can justify suppression activities that are both legal and illegal, or that ride the line between them.

I have anticipated several arenas of confusion regarding this narrative and its analysis. The first stems from who is related to whom. To clarify, in chapter 2 I detail connections among participants in the form of a list. A second problem involves individuals' names, some of which I have changed for the sake of confidentiality. It was no help that main supplier Juan Lococo and main dealer John Edwards both went by "John," although they also went by Big Man and Junior, respectively. They wound up as Lococo and Edwards in court documents, and I generally refer to them as Lococo or Big Man and Edwards or Junior in writing. Kevin Allen similarly could go by Kevin, Allen, or K-Rok. Though I often talk to the person I know as Kevin on the phone, I instead chose to write mostly about K-Rok. As for Charlotte Jackson, Tina was her family's pet name for her; the Fly was the streets'. And Tina herself spared no imaginative twist when providing names to the police, as evidenced by the list of aliases that begins this book. Multiple names are an age-old tactic of resistance in areas with high levels of state intrusion. But they are also a function of changing contexts and relationships. My ultimate decision was to try to stick to one name, even though one name fails to represent the multiple relationships and time periods in which persons and names operate.

The third arena of confusion has to do with the courts. Federal sentencing laws are labyrinthine. Even the neatest part about them—the sentencing guidelines—twists through zones, levels, and categories, all of which run concurrently. It's a tidy thing on paper, but spare anyone who attempts to render it in prose.[39]

Each of the five chapters introduces or explores different characters, examines particular social issues, and tells a story that runs, for the most part, chronologically. Chapter 1, "The Game," is about the drug trade and the play of surveillance efforts in the two neighborhoods. It introduces FBI special agent Rob King, as well as the main cocaine supplier Juan Lococo and key informant Crystal. In it I look at the inception of the case and the use of surveillance strategies, including confidential informants and wiretaps. I discuss the manner in which these tactics erode trust and informal networks of control, even while performing police work aimed at protecting community members.

Chapter 2, "Charlotte's Web," explores gang members' crime-family networks as sites of power and pathology. The family is an immensely malleable symbol and an even more complicated daily reality for people living at the nexus of poverty and criminality. Authorities can never quite settle on what kind of symbol the family should be. Despite their emphasis on the corruption, dysfunction, or weakness of the family, they also sever from familial situations the consequences of broader economic changes, suppression, and incarceration. This chapter attempts to realign contexts and outcomes through the stories, opinions, and reflections of Operation Fly Trap families shaped in part by multigenerational involvement in crime. In particular, I explore the relationships between Tina and Junior's daughter, Tawana, and Tawana's godson, Tink Tink. To this end, I examine the otherwise unpublicized moments of kinship, socialization, and storytelling that partially informed Operation Fly Trap. I contrast the viewpoints of family members and law enforcement to examine constructions of precision, disorder, necessity, and materialism that together attempt to exert a measure of control over ghetto environments.

Chapter 3, "Broken Families," presents the stories of several family members behind the sweep targets. Their narratives frame a discussion of collateral damage to the families of incarcerated people. Unintended consequences include threatened or actual eviction, the involvement of child social services, destabilization of families, depression in children, and high mortality rates among already vulnerable people (women, in this case). This chapter argues that suppression activities are a form of structural violence, which leads to increased poverty rates, negative health outcomes, and instability among the families of those targeted. Together, these findings demonstrate that police work inadvertently damages the family networks that would, if strengthened, provide the best crime prevention available.

Chapter 4, "Cutting the Head off the Snake," weighs policing strategies against the structure and culture of gang membership. I analyze data on gang violence before and after the Fly Trap task force and ask what difference the removal of twenty-eight individuals from two problem neighborhoods made in terms of combating gang violence and the drug trade. I discuss the origin of some of the violence in this area, issues of gang leadership, several key deaths, and the evolution of two important characters: Kevin Allen and Mark Brooks. By exploring the relationship between the drug trade and rampant neighborhood violence, I examine whether the drug trade is an effective mechanism through which to pursue violent individuals. The goal of this chapter is to create a more nuanced portrait of the relationship among gang violence, the drug trade, and state suppression.

The final chapter, "The Prosecutor's Darling," analyzes drug conspiracy charges against several of the twelve people who were tried together in *United States v. Edwards*. The manner in which Tina, Tawana, Kevin, Lococo, and Junior all come to terms with their sentences leads to discussion of the legal charge of conspiracy, the 100:1 crack versus powder cocaine disparity, mental health and substance abuse issues related to incarceration, religion behind bars, as well as the practice of giving information to lessen sentences. The examples demonstrate how breaches in people's interpretation of the courts lead to accusations of unverifiable governmental wrongdoing and eminently verifiable governmental injustice. I was never able to interview the lawyers on either side of this case. Focused entirely on the courts, chapter 5 does not represent law enforcement perspectives as strongly as do previous chapters.

The book concludes with the legal argument "fruit of the poison tree," and I use it as a metaphor to discuss the Fly Trap story. In the Fly Trap case as well as countless others, fruit of the poison tree argues that evidence obtained from tainted methods should also be considered tainted. Here, the poison tree is a metaphor for the overreliance on punitive methods to solve social problems. Repeated in conclusion is the larger argument that incarceration can lead to increased poverty rates, negative health outcomes, rises in violence, and instability among already vulnerable families. The conclusion also returns to the symbolic importance of manufacturing gangs as iconic, newly federalized villains and updates the reader on the lives of key Fly Trap characters.

CHAPTER ONE

The Game

Juan Emanuel Lococo, also known as Bigman, hadn't been raised limited, as the rest of his eight siblings in Los Angeles had. If anything, he had been spoiled by his grandparents, who doted on his sister and him. When John was sixteen, things began to change. His grandfather lost the use of his arms and legs in a car accident, and someone clapped a mysterious $500 lien on their Pomona home. No one knew what it was for. John's grandmother kept it a secret from the family. By the time John's grandfather died two years later, the bank had foreclosed on the house, and John's grandmother died within months of moving out.

John dreamed of somehow buying back the house for his family. One day he approached the people who now lived there and asked if they would sell his boyhood home to him. They refused. Somehow, he promised his mother, he would reclaim it as a surprise for her. He made the decision to deal drugs in sheer ignorance, he says now. He didn't know about community college or legitimate work opportunities. He only knew that he was tired of people saying no to his family. John swore they would never have to endure his grandparents' shame and hardship. "I'm gonna make sure of it," he told his family. Any time they needed help, he would be there for them.

John was not drawn to the drug trade because of the violence, he said, but because of the practicality of it. He wanted the money. He was watching a television news show about a drug cartel in Mexico when the idea clicked. After he arrived in Sonora, the city profiled as a hub of the Mexican drug trade, a man in what later would become the Sinaloa cartel befriended him. Quick trust was based on the fact that John reminded the cartel man of someone who had taken care of him long ago, when he was a young farm worker in the United States. This uncanny similarity opened the cartel to Lococo. Half Italian and half Mexican, John became known as El Gionni, El Italiano, or sometimes, El Loko de L.A. He developed a reputation for being trustworthy and dependable, someone who gave and got respect. The words of his grandparents rang in his ears: "My grandfather would tell me, 'Always make sure people respect you; *make* them respect you.' When he was out of earshot, my grandmother would quietly tell me, '*Mijo*, never confuse respect with fear. May people respect you, and if they do, you'll see that they will have *cariño* for you as well. Never make people fear you.'" During John's days among the cartels, there was *cariño* for the narcos. They were like Robin Hood figures: for the people, and against the government where it fell short. The narcos' revolutionary edge carried over from their Sinaloese heritage, which combined valor with violence. "You see, people in Culiacán, or even Sinaloa in general, like to say working against the government is being *Sinaloense*. It's your inheritance."[1] It was unusual for an outsider to be accepted into the tight-knit drug families of Mexico, but the capos soon realized that John, eager to prove himself, would take on work no one else was willing to do.

In the early 1990s, many cartels remained friendly, with kin ties and compadre connections. Lethal violence in Mexico was limited to a fracture between the northern Tijuana cartel and the southern Sinaloa cartel. Little of the dismemberment, humiliation, rape, or kidnapping of today marked intercartel warfare back then. "I mean, we killed, but when we did, where they fell was where it ended. Before, we *never* extorted; we *never* kidnapped." No dumping bodies in front of churches or schools. "Today," John says, "there is no *cariño* for the narcos."

In the early 1990s, the Sinaloa bosses gave John increasing responsibility. Eventually they offered him a *plaza* to control, an offer that carried with it the subtext "kill or be killed." John declined. He was growing into two people, he says. First was the one his grandmother had raised and nurtured, the one who would buy all the kids in town leather shoes, just so they would have something to put on their feet. That first one wanted to be a father, a grandfather, a son, an uncle, a brother. Second was the one who never slept well, who was "worried" constantly—about cops, business, enemies, past actions, possible futures. Juan Emanuel Lococo had developed a distaste for violence.

Lococo wound up serving time in a Mexican prison, where he occupied himself by planning a return to California. Back home, Lococo became a major distributor of powder cocaine to the gangs of South Central L.A. "Sales and distribution was something I could do without so much guilt,"

he says. "Rule number one about sales and distribution: violence and killings equal no sales or low sales. A whole new set of rules." He and his
family still lived in modest, working-class houses, in the heart of a South
Central gang neighborhood. But at least they had houses.

By the time the cartel offered him a wider piece of business stateside,
Lococo knew eyes were on him. He didn't know it was King and the FBI,
but he knew someone was there. He stalled the cartel in Mexico, who now
wanted him to peddle China White heroin, a drug so pure you could snort
it like cocaine. He left the bosses with a promise that he would return
to Mexico in three months to follow a new path. At just two and a half
months in, Operation Fly Trap interrupted his plans.

The FBI had cut Lococo loose from the 38th Street task force. Everyone knew about him, but no one could quite finger him. Lococo, however,
soon resurfaced during Operation Fly Trap. The task force had supposedly
connected him to their case by accident, but questions arose later about
whether Fly Trap had been a fishing expedition to net him as a specific
target. Lococo was a standout supplier in a sea of otherwise indistinguish-
able dealers and curb servers. The others, especially Tina, were pawns. He
was the big cheese, and he was convinced he had been screwed. They all
were convinced of it. In their eyes, they in no way merited the punishment
they got, just for peddling drugs.

The Villain Big Head was the connection to Lococo through his brother-
in-law, Ricky. Ricky was Lococo's right-hand man who supplied drugs to
the Pueblos and Villains. In the beginning, Big Head hooked John Edwards up with Ricky, who introduced Ricky to Tina, then Tina to Lococo. Tina was the only one aside from the FBI who ever called Lococo
"Bigman." Through Bigman, Tina would arrange packages for Junior,
K-Rok, and herself, and all three would distribute them to members of the
Pueblos, Villains, and in some cases the Black P. Stones—another Bloods
gang—to deal on the streets. This arrangement was mutually beneficial,
and those higher up the ladder imposed "taxes" on those lower down so
that, as Tina says, "everybody could make their little profit."

On U.S. streets, the colloquial term for the drug trade is "the game."
People in the game sometimes respond to queries regarding their profession by stating that they cook "chickens" or "birds." Chefs for the post-
Fordist era, they cook up a grand recipe of two parts powder, one part
baking soda. They add a little water and heat gently until off-white paste
becomes the rock called a "dub" or "dove." They locate a spot to wait for
customers who often look jacked-up and pathetic. The chefs' jockeying to
serve these customers can look equally jacked up and pathetic.

The game gets much of its energy from the play of surveillance: the chase, cat-and-mouse, and moves on the chessboard. The players are somewhat more diversified in this game: growers, manufacturers, transporters, suppliers, dealers, servers, addicts, cops, agents, snitches, wires, GPS units, computers, and confidential sources. All kinds of new possibilities for social integration and disintegration emerge from the combination of these parts.

Within the game, higher-level businesspersons like Juan Lococo or John Edwards generally manufacture a buffer between themselves and the streets through other key individuals. In the case of *United States v. Edwards*, the key individual was Tina Fly. When Junior and K-Rok wanted packages, they trusted only Tina. They would call her, and she would get the money to take to Bigman. She called herself the middleman, trusted in part, she said, because she was a woman. Junior trusted her, Rok trusted her, and Bigman trusted her. They did not necessarily know or trust each other. Tina was the linchpin, the only one to connect each and every individual in the case. She was the safeguard between the two Johns and the streets.

Regular street-level drug peddlers seldom have a Tina. They have no luxury to sit it out behind the scenes while others do their bidding. For them, the streets themselves serve as the most powerful asset against law enforcement scrutiny.

The Villains' neighborhood, for example, is typical of South Central L.A. with its rows of old Victorian houses or bungalows with dead lawns or rose gardens, stucco covering original wood, and iron fences to keep dogs and kids in, and intruders out. While dealing is frequently done outside, hiding is best done inside, hence the trope of the crack house where the streets transform domestic space into a partially secluded drug zone. On the streets, close scrutiny of cars and strangers, intimate knowledge of neighborhood networks, and encoded systems of communication enable secrecy and illegality to persist despite repeated law-enforcement intrusions.

The Pueblo del Rio housing development, just north and east of the Villains' neighborhood, combines local knowledge with an insular built environment. Federally subsidized and originally built as World War II housing, the development enjoys secluded play areas, mature eucalyptus trees, and afternoon breezes. The development was codesigned by Richard Neutra, who worked with a team of modern architects, including Paul Williams, a prominent African American architect. The Pueblos are low slung with many inward-facing units.[2] Neutra's idea had been that building beautiful, well-designed spaces would make for contented, healthy communities. Life in L.A.'s projects would disprove much of this thesis; after just two generations, the developments became hotbeds of gangs and crime. But Neutra wasn't entirely wrong. Most project communities are village-like. Young children can safely pal around on the common playgrounds under the collective eye of many mothers, whereas in the Villains' or other non-project neighborhoods, individual caregivers must keep a closer watch.

The seclusion that provides the children of the projects with safety during play also shelters more nefarious activities. The trick here is to locate a place out of the punitive public eye, to take advantage of the natural contours of the units and the semiprivate streets used to reach them. Outsiders' attempts to intrude upon this space are a much trickier business.

In the Pueblos, four sets of rail lines separate the big and little sides of the projects. When it was first built, a lavender metal-and-concrete overpass protecting the kids from having to cross the tracks was host to a flasher. At first kids didn't use the overpass for fear they would be stuck, unable to escape his open coat. They hid from him by continuing to cross the tracks that had already claimed one of their number.[3] Pueblo Bishops also felt the gaze of someone upon them. Like the children, they paid attention to new elements in the neighborhood, to strangers, unusual cars, and changes in the behavior of those they knew. They began strategically shooting out streetlights and blocking specific drug-dealing streets with the gigantic black trashcans of the projects. On the night police killed a homie named Wolf Loc, the Pueblos moved a few of the massive receptacles onto the Blue Line tracks in protest. And daily the cans served another purpose: to cordon off the drug mainlines of the projects. The Pueblos knew people were watching. They fought back with darkness and dead ends.

In this manner, gangs like the Pueblo Bishops and Blood Stone Villains perform their own forms of surveillance and control of neighborhood territories. By exploiting the structural idiosyncrasies of built environments and by appropriating space for their own use, gangs contest the state's authority through criminal enterprise. They make neighborhoods into their own sovereign zones, with rules of law, regimes of discipline, and an economy that sits in place. Although they may not be overtly de-facto political, these processes highlight the state's and gangs' incomplete control over these territories. The entities of gang and state are thus uncomfortable partners in a game they must be content to win only partially.

As if mirroring the projects in which they grew, the Five Duse Pueblo

Bishops Bloods were a gang cops always considered difficult to pene-trate.[4] Law enforcement tried to have undercover officers jumped into the gang—a tactic that had been successful elsewhere. They tried to get people to deal to undercover officers both there and in the Blood Stone Villains neighborhood. According to Officer Brooks, "You know the Vil-lains were violent, but the Pueblos were way more violent as far as putting work in. They got more structure down there. Pueblos is different. I mean those guys are born to the projects. Most of the guys on the Villains side, those dudes own their homes. The project people is, would you say a more poor class of people, and they got more problems." As a result of the nur-tured self-protection, hands-on police tactics lost to thirty years of Pueblo history and paranoia.

The FBI created a litany of failures on the surveillance front to justify the wiretap warrants that would become keys to breaking open the full reach of the conspiracies. When the FBI or LAPD would drive through the neighborhood, for example, people would ID their cars. The Pueblos had a contact at the DMV; officers suspected this person might be giving up the feds' vehicle information. When marks saw a conspicuous car, they would frequently make obscene gestures, curse, or otherwise indicate that the officers' cover had been blown, again.

Much to the chagrin of authorities, John Edwards's apartment faced the back of the complex, not the street. Edwards's sister waved at the sur-veillance team one day as she drove by in a white Cadillac. On a different day, a group of Pueblos flashed gang signs at Special Agent Moreno and LAPD detective Murphy, and one of the gang members patted his front to signify that he was armed. On another occasion, after a conveniently timed arrest, a girl came up to the surveillance vehicle in the Villains' neighborhood and knocked on its tinted windows. Agents tried placing "surreptitious tracking devices" on K-Rok's and Tina Fly's cars. K-Rok discovered his immediately, and Tina removed hers within two weeks. The devices fell short of the more clandestine operations the teams had hoped for: aside from the constant risk of premature discovery, the device had a battery that required regular changing, which was hard to do on the down low. Agents also had to drive in close proximity to the cars for the devices to work. After scrapping the units, the team thought about look-ing through people's trash. Separating personal from communal trash in shared dumpsters proved a logistical nightmare, and this tactic yielded al-most no results. Narcotics trafficking seemed to leave little in the way of a paper trail, and in at least one later instance a wiretap picked up Tina telling Black to put incriminating trash into a store's receptacle instead of her own.

Within such constrained surveillance contexts, the agents were always on the look out for potential informers by sampling the waters here, prodding a bit there. They decided they needed to place someone inside the projects—preferably someone who was already a known element. Authorities found it impossible to do surveillance properly on a gang so impenetrable, in a complex designed to be so insular. They took what they could get.

A crack addict and prostitute named Crystal became Confidential Source 1 and Operation Fly Trap's golden girl. The FBI planted CS-1 in a unit of the Pueblo del Rio projects. She wore a wire and recorded drug transactions with several major individuals, including Tina Fly. She arranged a key purchase of powder cocaine for $14,500 and also gave information about the structure of the Pueblo Bishops gang. Crystal was, for a time, the lone finger pointing in the direction of John Edwards as high command of the local drug trade.

In a neighborhood of poor people, Crystal was even poorer. She used to clean people's houses. She babysat, and had done so for several of the Fly Trap targets when they were kids. Tina used to donate her clothes and shoes to Crystal and would sometimes give her money. Tina and Crystal had done drugs together in the mid- to late 1990s, at the height of Tina's addictions. They had run the streets together, prostituting on Central Avenue. They had lived together as lovers for a time. Crystal had also exchanged sex for drugs with most of the targets in the case. According to Tina, Crystal had once been on the ten most-wanted list. Indeed, when the U.S. attorneys presented CS-1's criminal record in court, the counts against her ranged from vandalism to felony murder.

During Fly Trap, Crystal had a boyfriend who was a "baller" named Frankie. Frankie owned a bookie joint, and his solvency made him stand out on the street. It also made Crystal's rather large drug purchases seem unremarkable. As the key informant, CS-1 used her existing knowledge to attempt to score drugs. Still an addict, she now had another monkey on her back: simultaneous listening and recording by law enforcement to document her drug purchases. She put herself on the line for pay, a job with which she had grown well acquainted. She was first paid $200, then $500 more. After that came separate transactions for which she was given $250, $250, and $350, respectively. Finally came the $12,000 for relocation. Of the six confidential sources formally involved in the federal case, only CS-1 was willing to testify in court. Four of the six other confidential sources attempted drug transactions or wore a wire, and the remaining two provided some information but refused further involvement.

Law enforcement's ability to locate insiders like CS-1 who will talk or set up others—preferably while wearing a wire—is critical because of the spatial and behavioral challenges of doing gang and drug surveillance. Marrying the snitch to the wire weds the jacked up and pathetic to the sanctity of the machine: the one is compromised and generally desperate, the other, sanitary and unfeeling. This is no easy marriage to broker. Its yentas are people like Brooks and King—individuals with experience, connections, and knowledge of the law. They find and flip, they coerce and cajole, they threaten and outfit, they predict and outwit.

FBI special agent Robert King knew a lot about nurturing informants. He had come from a law enforcement family. He remembered the "itty, bitty Indian dolls" that his FBI father had brought back from a months-long stint at Wounded Knee in the early 1970s when King was a kid. After serving as an agent, his dad had become a regular cop who instilled the virtues of honesty, equality, and integrity in his son. King's first job was with the Mississippi sheriff's department, but he later moved into casino security for the higher pay. He soon lost the stomach for drunken behavior, however, and took a position with the Mississippi Department of Corrections as chief of internal affairs. His family was required to live on the state penitentiary's grounds. His wife, Lea Ann, said that she "was bawling when we moved there . . . . But when we left, I was bawling because it was such a wonderful family." After a year of internal affairs work, King and his team indicted over fifty guards involved in various corrupt activities. "It's a different kind of violation," he says. "How can you expect the inmates to do right when the guards aren't doing what they're supposed to do?" At the penitentiary, King learned how to nurture trust without coercion:

> When you're in those units, you're in there without guns or anything else. And those inmates, it's not like the threat of going to jail will get anybody to talk to you, because they're already in prison. So you have to learn how to talk to them, and get people to tell you what you need. That was the biggest thing, just learning how to deal with people. And there was a lot of people that couldn't walk in certain areas, because sometimes, unfortunately, the inmates throw things at you. But I've always been taught you treat everybody the same. So I never had any issues.

Rob King had been an FBI special agent since 1998 and had come to Los Angeles in 1999. In L.A., he had immersed himself in a world of violence, gangs, and drugs. These dangers did not present new threats to him. King had tackled the drug trade as a deputy sheriff in Mississippi. He had extensive training and field experience, had learned the slang, and understood the way drug dealers work.

Lessons learned during the early period of his career provided King with a solid foundation for Fly Trap. In turn, his skill level provided Fly Trap with a stand-up agent who gave and got respect from participants. King sometimes told informers, "You don't need to do this. If you can't handle being around drugs cause you're doing good right now, you don't need to do this." Nothing for King was personal. He followed the law and wanted to make sure other people did, too. He remembered his father's words: "Whatever you do, you have to be able to look at yourself in the mirror every morning."

King had never met anyone as good at nurturing informants as LAPD officer Mark Brooks. Brooks had more people in the field calling him than anyone King had ever seen. When the two would drive around, Brooks's cell phone would ring multiple times a day. "I don't know who that was," Brooks would say, "but they said that . . . " and off the pair would go. King knew a number of people in the neighborhood disliked Brooks, but he recognized that Brooks's aggressive demeanor was a form of self-protection.

Broad-scale criminal investigations in hostile circumstances require continuous patterns of apprehension, coercion, and information gathering. Individuals who decide to cooperate may receive payment for their information or absolution from their guilt.[5] The idea that such informers are unknown and impartial, confidential and reliable, is countered by the reality that many, like CS-1, are drug addicts; are known to the community; have set up people for money; often have long-standing ties in the neighborhood that can skew their testimony; and are either manipulated by the state to serve its ends or are using the system to manipulate their way around charges against themselves.

Alexandra Natapoff, an L.A.-based legal scholar, has spent much of her career analyzing how snitching contributes to community erosion. Although snitches technically work with law enforcement to increase public safety, Natapoff calls snitches "a communal liability." She writes that they "increase crime and threaten social organization, interpersonal relationships, and socio-legal norms in their home communities, even as they are tolerated or under-punished by law enforcement because they are useful."[6] The number of young African American males under the supervision of the justice system is high (one in five), as is the pressure exerted upon them to snitch. Such snitches contribute to community mistrust and the breakdown of insider control networks.

Similar forms of mistrust and dissolution also carry familial consequences. When Juan Lococo's stepfather, Angel, was arrested on state charges for possession of a kilo of cocaine, the police pressured him to give up information about his stepson. Lococo's name kept coming up— too much, it seemed to Angel—and Angel knew he had to warn Lococo somehow. Angel called his wife from the jailhouse phone and told her to tell Lococo that, next time he was in Mexico, could he buy him a pair of those tire-tread sandals? This request issued the warning that Lococo should high tail it out of town, and had he taken it seriously Lococo might have escaped. But he thought the police were just trying to scare Angel. Lococo knew that someone was watching him and that earlier in the year the FBI had not arrived by chance in a small Mexican town he'd frequented. He knew that odd things were happening. When his truck reappeared after mysteriously vanishing for a few days, the folks at the car dealership seemed nervous when Lococo went to retrieve it. According to Lococo, those few days would have provided the FBI with ample opportunity to have the vehicle outfitted with a GPS tracking device.

Whereas Angel tried to warn Lococo about the police's interest in him, Lococo's brother-in-law Ricky did the opposite. Ricky had worked with Lococo as a dealer, and the two supplied cocaine to members of the Pueblo Bishops. Lococo had bought Ricky a car, a sign of his trust. But at some point, the feds flipped Ricky. Ricky told them that Lococo imported large quantities of drugs from Mexico, and that his wife—Ricky's sister— had also been involved. He told of secret compartments both in Lococo's truck and his mother's kitchen. The border patrol stopped Lococo every time he crossed into the United States, jacked his truck off the ground, and searched every nook and cranny. They never found any drugs, though they knew he had cartel connections.

A short time before the arrests, Ricky skipped town and supposedly took a bus to Mexico. By then, little question remained within the family about Ricky's role as a snitch. Court documents show that a niggling doubt remained about Lococo's stepfather: a tiny notation in Lococo's handwriting next to the anonymous Confidential Source 2 reads, "Angel?"[7] Angel was not CS-2, who police later identified as a member of the Pueblo Bishops gang, but for a time suspicion colored their relationship.

Family and gang, as combined entities, have a predictably strong relationship in crime that the pervasiveness of informants both cements and tests. Here, within one family, two members were pressured to turn state's evidence. The federal war on drugs has encouraged this kind of information getting and in the process has turned family members against one another. The prevalence of snitching as a police tactic puts strain on these families, in particular because kinship, if not friendship, must signify whom one can trust. Most brotherly rituals in gangs are simulacra of kinship, and both fictive and blood connections are directly related to the manufacture of trust within gangs. As surveillance and snitching create divisions within families and neighborhoods, they contribute to a general lack of trust that elevates the threat of violence against suspect individuals to the most successful manner of information control.

From the criminal perspective, people become informational liabilities every time they come into direct contact with the law. After three Villains were arrested one day, Tina called to let Junior know that they, a gun, some checks, and "some blow" had been taken in.

> "And how long ago this been?" Junior asked.
> "Shit, today."
> "See now, now some of them motherfuckers just need to keep they mouth shut."
> "Exactly."
> "You know what I mean?"
> "That's where I'm at with that shit."
> "Yup. Motherfuckers need to, need to just keep they mouth closed."

As with the three Villains, those with direct connections to the network become security risks when arrested. People with peripheral connections, such as neighborhood residents or addicts, are both risks and necessities. Their knowledge can be as intimate as that of a gang member without as strong a complication of compromised loyalty. Risk and trust fit hand in glove in gang culture and in law enforcement relationships with snitches. Both must balance unknowable quantities of risk and trust to survive in the game.

Snitching is not a one-size-fits-all enterprise. Some people flatly refuse to give information. Others give a little and then stop. Some agree to engage in a certain act—to wear a wire and set somebody up, for example—and then find they cannot go through with it. Police call this "going sideways." Yet others pretend to agree with law enforcement and then make misleading statements.

"Backdoor snitches," also known as "dry snitches" "pretend they're not snitching when they really are," as one man told me. They do this by not quite saying a name but by making a culprit's identity abundantly clear. "Wet snitching," also called "hard snitching," generally describes a fully cooperating informant for law enforcement.

Attempts to control information in the neighborhood range from stigma and exclusion to violence. One wiretapped conversation between Tina's boyfriend K-Rok and Cece, another Pueblo del Rio resident, revealed the deeply gendered interpretation of snitching at the community level. This followed a longer discussion of how ignorant K-Rok had been about police surveillance regarding his particular unit. Cece urged K-Rok to lay low in the projects for at least three weeks, and she further speculated that any arrests made might lead back to information about him:

CECE: You know, motherfuckers be talking to they . . . probably took somebody else to jail and been like, you know what I'm saying, who be over there, woo, woo, woop, you know. Even though them your homies, you know what I'm saying?

ROK: Them niggas ain't my homies.

CECE: But ohhh, and then that nigga be like woo, woo, woop, you know, say your name or something—just to get him out of trouble.

ROK: Yeah, yeah. Niggas do that all the time.

CECE: Yeah, niggas do that. And bitches. Especially, shit, bitch ass niggas been doing that.

ROK: Specially niggas.

CECE: All the time though.

ROK: Specially niggas, cause they go to jail more than bitches.

The conversation moved from a generalized discussion of surveillance to how people, particularly fellow homies, give information when arrested. Whereas women (bitches) may be more prone to snitching, men (niggas) more frequently enter temptation to snitch because of their higher incarceration rate. "Bitch ass nigga" generally refers to a man with such effeminate characteristics as talking a lot. Bitch ass niggas have compromised masculinity, fluid loyalty, are unable to stand up for themselves, and might back down or run away from a fight. Here, "woo, woo, woop" is a street slang gloss for all kinds of conversation.

Gang loyalty in African American neighborhoods has eroded in recent years. The war on drugs has raised sentencing stakes much higher for those charged and has disproportionately targeted blacks. Mandatory minimum sentences, particularly for crack cocaine, mean that those convicted serve more time for less crime. Snitching has long been the only way around these mandatory minimum sentencing laws. Since the advent of the war on drugs, plentiful snitch work has made giving up information on one's homies a regularized, if vilified, part of life for gang members and others involved in the drug trade.

Unlike the wet, dry, hard, or backdoor snitch, the person who does not snitch is a "real gangsta," "solid," "a good dude," "a stand up guy," "straight," or "keepin' it gangster."[8] If you crack and snitch, you've crossed a line that can never be redrawn, even if you have a change of heart: "in the long run they're still no good or a rat, and can wind up pushing up daisies anyway. There is no making that shit up on my side of the tracks," as one man told me. People on the ground, however, may find it difficult to determine a person's status. In crime-prone neighborhoods, most assume they cannot trust those around them, in the same way they assume they cannot talk on a phone that might be tapped. Despite snitches' association with law enforcement, they introduce another element of disorder to the neighborhood.

Within this framework, snitches cross a dangerous border between social worlds as human conduits of information. They go where the state cannot and often risk their lives to do so. Neighborhood residents describe what amounts to the backstabbing of close relatives and friends as deeply emasculating, promotive of violent grabs for control over leaks, and morally out of step with a gang culture rooted in an earlier area.

One day Tina was driving through the projects by Crystal's unit and saw that several Pueblos had surrounded Crystal and were shouting at her.

Tina pulled over and opened her car door. "Come in, Crystal, what's going on?"

"They trying to jump me!" Crystal screamed to her friend.

Tina said, "Girl, come on, get in this car," and Crystal dove in. They drove to the safety of the other side of the tracks, leaving the Pueblos for the time with their discovery: surveillance equipment in Crystal's closet.

A few days later, Rok told Tina what had happened with Crystal. A betrayal that deep made no sense to her. She simply could not believe it.

I'm the one kind of saved her life. If it wasn't for me, over there that day to get her, they were gonna do her right there. I still ask myself, how could she do me like that? Out of all . . . you know I give her clothes. I feed her, help her out, you know? We was on drugs at the same time. Cause I had been knowing her for so long. And they paid her. Then she was on drugs the whole time. I mean, how could they let her? She doing all this. And they steady setting people up. You got her to come in. You know, they talking about they couldn't get none of they federal agents to come in and get too close. Cause they were scared. Gang members gonna kill them or shoot them, they were too violent. But y'all let her get in the projects, with the camera, in the building, and set 'em up. I'm like, those feds don't care who they use, they just use anybody. Then my friends are like, y'all wanna do something to her? I'm like, no. Uh uh. God'll take care of her. You know. Let her go.

CS-1 had been paid for her dealings and the risks she'd taken, but now she was scared. She wanted out of the informer business.

After this incident, Crystal continued to wear a wire for the feds despite her fears. And Tina continued to sell drugs to her. "I didn't believe it," Tina says, "and I kept dealing with her. That's how she still had me, how she played me. To this day it's like, why didn't I stop?" Tina says that, knowing what she knows now, she should have left Crystal to her fate with the Pueblos that day.

Some of Crystal's stranger behavior now made sense: her continual offers, for example, to allow Tina and others to use her unit as a base. (An FBI-controlled crack house certainly is any special agent's dream come true.) Crystal also extracted from gang members the meaning of their lingo. Between what Crystal told authorities and the transactions she orchestrated, Crystal helped sentence many targets not only under the purview of Fly Trap but all over the east side during that period.

Despite Tina's talk about wishing she had left Crystal to her fate that day in the projects, Tina maintains a long-distance buffer around Crystal.

To be honest with you, like I told my family and my friends, don't mess with her. God'll take care of her. I didn't want revenge like that. I know my life is . . . is pretty messed up right now. I feel what goes around comes around, you know. And God wouldn't work for me if I had something done to her. So I don't have that much hatred to where I have to have something done to her. Cause I want God to still bless me. I'm trying to change my life over to the better. And it ain't just me who she did wrong, she did wrong to a lot of people.

The FBI relocated Crystal, but she continues to frequent the neighborhood, "still running the streets, still on drugs," as Tina says. Law enforcement has cut her loose and deemed her too unreliable to work for them. Tina says, "I guess it's by the grace of God that she's still alive." That, and by the grace of Tina Fly.

*   *   *

Far from confidential, Crystal's identity, along with the identities of other confidential sources in the case, is well known to the community. Indeed, this is the only reason I have been able to write about them in such detail. These informants' roles in the Fly Trap case have earned them animosity or forgiveness on a sliding scale. The animosity stems from the use of violence to control the flow of drug-related information, but the forgiveness stems from the common knowledge of the system's profound flaws. People in the neighborhoods have repeatedly told me how scandalous they consider the use of informers to be, what they see as authorities' exploitation of the weak, such as drug addicts like Crystal, and how the constant threat of inappropriately long federal sentences is a worry for those who don't cooperate.

"Meat Man," or Confidential Reliable Informant 1, used to cruise around the neighborhood selling pilfered goods to finance his heroin addiction. Sometimes he'd unload a television for ten dollars, but his most reliable money came from "cattle rustling," selling sausages and steaks stolen from the supermarket. According to state target Ben Kapone's mother, Linda, the LAPD used Meat Man's unfortunate decision to shoot up in a local nature park to recruit him. Like Crystal, the LAPD paid him to wear a wire and record drug transactions. I met Meat Man while he was washing Ben's car at one of the units. He offered to wash my car as well for five dollars but was so messed up that instead he threw up in the gutter.

A few days after the takedown, Ben's mother ran into Meat Man at the store. She confronted him, but he fled. The proprietor told her that Meat Man had turned in other people from the neighborhood as well and had already been relocated. Later, in court, the task force suggested it give up the identity of the confidential informant to further the case against Ben. But what was there to give up? His identity was no longer secret within the community. After the bust, Ben's mom would periodically run into Meat Man in the neighborhood, dutifully reporting it to me every time. "I saw Dan again today." Or, "Guess who I saw at the store yesterday?"

About two years after the sweep, Ben (who had already served his time) and his wife ran into Meat Man at the store. Meat Man failed to recognize him right away, but they exchanged polite greetings, "Wha's up, my brotha?" etc. When Ben responded by using the man's old moniker, Meat Man began to panic, make excuses, and say that he hadn't wanted to set Ben up, but the feds had forced him to do it. Ben said of the FBI after this encounter, "They don't have no feelings for these dudes. They just let them live they little lifestyle. They just don't give a fuck about them. What if I had been the type of person who was out for revenge? He wouldn't be here right now."

Crystal's or Meat Man's community exposure is a chronic problem in a system that promises but does not bring anonymity to those who aid law enforcement. Although legal documents that formally reveal the identities of cooperating individuals remain sealed, finding out through courtroom discovery that includes recorded transactions is not difficult. According to Tina Fly, "When you read discovery, you play that tape back in your head. On this certain day, you met CS-1, CS-2 was X. And I know who said that. So by me reading, it kind of like, tell you everything, who got arrested this day, who could have said that. You know, it's just a little common sense, that it'll tell you." Informants cannot act as tools for social change either in the lives of individuals or in the lives of communities because the strength of structural violence, poverty, and the effects of prison in disenfranchising people is so great. Snitches do, however, help to put people in jail, and they selectively feed the authorities information. By so doing, snitches also create paranoia, undermine trust within neighborhoods, and to a degree have made gangs more unpredictable as they struggle to combat changes within their culture wrought from without.

Law enforcement's conduct sometimes seems to verge on pure manipulation when agencies flip people like Crystal or Meat Man by holding prison time and addiction over their heads. Officers, however, have a different story to tell. Many like Brooks understand the unintended consequences of policing strategies such as the use of confidential sources. To them, "snitch" is a dirty word, one that has an unflattering critique built into it. Officers want people to cooperate with their enforcement efforts in order to increase public safety. To encourage cooperation represents an offer to aid, at least in some measure, the good guys in fighting gangs and drugs and the destruction both spread in communities. How are officers supposed to see into a culture so closed, where members have known one another all their lives? People don't call the police in those neighborhoods; they sometimes prefer to handle things on their own. Without the use of informers, authorities could never mount an effort like Operation Fly Trap.

Despite the confidential sources and their recorded transactions, the drug dealers continued to use their evasion experience to skirt the law. A higher level of the conspiracy remained just out of reach. Some of the informants were now afraid, particularly after Crystal's near miss with the Pueblos. One informer, after giving up information but refusing to testify in court, said he didn't want to die. Officers were also afraid of the violent ends they could meet during undercover work.

So Special Agent King compiled an affidavit that listed the challenges on the surveillance front. King cited the spatial difficulties, the fact that several of the confidential sources were incarcerated or not trusted by the gang members, and the fact that the sources as well as potential undercover officers were afraid of violent reprisal. The affidavit was exhaustive enough for a judge to grant the gold standard of surveillance, the Title III wiretap.

Title III wiretaps have authorized the surveillance of electronic communications since 1968. Originally, courts only granted such wiretaps in cases involving specific violent crimes, from hijackings to breaking into nuclear facilities. Today, courts use Title IIIs to disrupt and punish many kinds of criminal activity, including the trade in illegal drugs. A sworn affiant, like Special Agent King, must convince a judge that other forms of surveillance have been largely unsuccessful at achieving the goals of a case. In this instance King's affidavit persuaded the judge to authorize the taping of key Fly Trap targets' cellular phones. Although hard won, the authorization was almost guaranteed. In the history of Title III wiretaps from 1968 to 2005, judges have only denied 33 out of nearly 40,000 requests.[9]

Once the wiretaps were authorized, the case began to move at lightening speed. The feds heard Tina say she was going to get a gun from Tawana's house and shoot somebody. They hurried to the scene to disrupt her plans. Later, they discovered Tina's plans to pay off a mental health worker to attest to her impaired mental health status as she faced a state drug case. They found out about the love triangle involving Black, Tina Fly, and K-Rok. They recorded many drug-related conversations between Tina Fly and Junior. And in one brief moment, they got Lococo: "Tina? This is Johnny, Bigman."

*   *   *

During this period, wiretaps were Special Agent King's job, 24/7. He lived and breathed them, immersing himself in the character and sensibility of ghetto life. The whole wiretap process was exhausting:

> People think the government can just turn on and listen to your phone. It is not like that. Because with those affidavits, oh god, they were long. And you have to do one every thirty days, and there are other documents you write through-out the thirty days to justify continuing. Just the administrative part of doing those parts is a nightmare. But if you have an active phone where you get a lot of calls like these were, it's almost like having your own TV crime drama. When you first start listening, you're trying to figure out who's who, who goes with what names, what are they talking about in code. For six months, that was our TV show that we watched everyday. When it was over, we all sat around and looked at each other, like, hey, they canceled our favorite show. It was almost like post-partum or something.

During the wiretap period, King's family rarely saw him. I asked him how his absence had impacted his relationships with his wife and kids. "What relationships?" he said. His wife only saw him coming and going, and he was practically a stranger to his son and young daughter. He would arrive home after everyone was in bed and leave before they got up in the morning. The family tried to carve out an afternoon or two on the week-end to be together, but Lea Ann considered herself a single parent dur-ing those times.

King had a monster commute from Riverside, part of which he shared with Mark Brooks. The pair used the drive in to hash out the specifics of the case and the drive home to unwind from the pressure built up over the day so they could walk through their respective doorways a little lighter.

Brooks and King were together so much that other members of the task force started jokingly referring to them as "Murtaugh and Riggs," the *Lethal Weapon* team.[10] On arrival in Westwood or at Newton Divi-sion station, they'd hole up with the other agents and officers, review the case with the assigned U.S. attorney, go over wiretap materials, or ven-ture into the field. People in the neighborhood would occasionally notice King, but they thought he was just some new white cop. Their hatred of Brooks, though, had a deep history. Whereas King maintained a respect-ful distance, with Brooks everything was personal. He was always in their face, always pushing his agenda, always repeating that he was "gonna get them someday."

In February 2003, a few months before the Fly Trap bust, Brooks and King were riding in a marked police car with fellow LAPD officer Tony Diaz. They saw several people standing in front of a house on 56th Street and recognized Nee-Nee Washington, Big Head's cousin, and the cousin of another Blood Stone Villains member, Erick Kennedy. The crowd scattered, and people began to yell obscenities at Officer Brooks. Later that same day, the team saw Nee-Nee walking outside of the neighborhood. They asked her if she would cooperate with the task force.

"Why would I want to give up my homies?" she asked.

Brooks said, "Because it would help the community."

"Fuck you," said Nee-Nee.

"Helping the community" to Nee-Nee Washington meant something entirely different than it did to Mark Brooks. Police rarely understand how they make the lives of people, even victims, more difficult by police involvement. Victims who have to go to court repeatedly, for example, sometimes lose their jobs. Other times they become, along with their families, targets of gang intimidation. For someone like Nee-Nee, herself a Fly Trap state target, "helping" the community would mean disregarding, using, and condemning the people closest to her in life: her family and friends.

Framed at the broader level of gang culture, the police are just one part of an equation that nurtures mistrust in urban areas. As Ben once put it, "The projects been went through so much snitching and chaos for so many years, they suspicious of everybody. It's not just the police, but other Bloods, other Crips, setting things up." Police exploit this suspicion in neighborhoods that already use mistrust as a cultural tactic. Instead of separating out police action or incarceration as anomalies, information getting weaves paranoia into the daily fabric of neighborhood life in a way unique among those who live in violence-prone areas.

Police surveillance in the neighborhood remains ghostly until officers take major action. Before arrests that justify neighborhood suspicions, people learn to manage persistent feelings of paranoia. Paranoia at the community level constitutes knowledge without power. At the individual level, paranoia lands people at the nexus of street smarts and simple insanity, bordering on the ridiculous, until the specter of what John Lococo's sister calls "something weird" is proven correct.

> "You know," my husband said, "there's something weird around here." I said, "Yeah, there is something weird." "You know, there's something weird." And he started going out there and observing. We just started seeing like different

things. I'm like, "No, but we always think like this." It was just our thin nerves, you know. Because before, other times, we would be like, "Why is this car here?" Or, "Why is *this* car here? There's something gonna happen." And everything would be false. So that day we didn't tell my brother nothing. And sometimes I feel guilty, but then again I'm like, no I shouldn't because my brother knew what he was doing and sooner or later he knew he was gonna get caught.

Those who failed to read the signs—to pay attention to their "thin nerves"—understand the divide between suspicion and knowledge, between what's possible and what a person can tangibly predict. They often consider suspicion something that, as in court, they ought to act upon only if it involves certainty beyond a reasonable doubt. Junior's sister Renee believes Tina's reluctance to act on her suspicions provided the police an opportunity to catch Junior.

She [Tina] knew, she knew something. She knew she was being followed. Tina used to tell her daughter something about police was on her, or she would see these polices watching her and it's like—well Mama why you won't tell? Why you didn't tell me the polices was on you or why you didn't let my dad know the police was following you like that because, by them following you, they came up on other folks doing other things. . . . And whatever my brother was doing illegal, they got into his works and they got to talking on their cell phones and all them cell phones was tapped and the house phone was tapped, the police watching everything.

During the Fly Trap investigation, compounding events in the neighborhoods led residents to believe that the police were watching or that snitches were active in the area. People were arrested and set free for no reason. Residents would notice unusual vehicles. But for the moment, Tina Fly, Junior, Lococo, Tawana, and the rest of the Fly Trap targets went about their business, attempting, as usual, to keep as low a profile as possible.

On June 20, 2003, Crystal received her money for relocation, and a few days later she began taunting people in the Blood Stone Villains neighborhood, handing out $100 bills and saying, "enjoy it while you can." The next morning, they found out what she meant.

CHAPTER TWO

Charlotte's Web

66 I remember that day like it was just yesterday," Tawana Edwards says. "Crystal kept saying, 'Y'all better be careful, they coming.' In that little, in her little voice."

Tawana had been in jail at the Metropolitan Detention Center in downtown L.A. for six months before she realized that the money Crystal had smugly doled out had come from the same people housing Tawana: the federal government. She and Big Head, who was also incarcerated at MDC, talked about it during visiting one day.

"Tawana," Big Head said, "you remember that day Crystal told us to be careful?" She did indeed. Since then her family and social units had been redefined as a drug-distribution conspiracy. She felt cut open.

When she was young Tawana had wanted to be just like her dad. Her mother—the woman she still calls "Tina" instead of "Mom"—constantly smoked drugs, and Tawana knew she didn't want to be like her. Tawana clearly remembers the day she took herself and her younger sister to live at their grandmother's house. It had been time for them to go someplace else, someplace safe, so she took her little sister, and they left.

Her father—whom she'd always called "Daddy" and not "Junior"—could by contrast do no wrong. His supportive presence outweighed Tawana's awareness that her dad was a drug dealer. She knew that if she had to choose one over the other—addiction versus dealing, mother versus father—Tawana would choose dealing and her father. "I would rather sell drugs than smoke 'em," Tawana says. "I wanted to be just like him."

Tawana came of age at her grandmother's house on 56th Street among many Blood Stone Villains who had grown up in multigenerational drug families. According to Tawana's grandmother, Genia Jackson, this was not an uncommon pattern in the neighborhood: "In this clientele, it's like a tradition most of the people in this area are involved in. Cause now, they mothers and they fathers, and they brothers and sisters sell drugs. The kids sell drugs and they kids are growing up and selling drugs. It's just a pattern. It's going in the same footsteps."

Big Head, legal name Dante Washington, came from another drug-oriented family. He had followed his mother and granny, both dealers, and begun dealing as a preteen. Ms. Jackson had known many dealers on her block when they were children. She had practically adopted Brian Favors, a.k.a. Redd, as she had many of the neighborhood kids. They were Tawana's compatriots. Her household might have sheltered Tawana from their influence if Tawana had sought such protection. When Tawana got out of federal prison, she would rarely leave her grandma's house in an effort to stay clean. On the cusp of adolescence, however, Tawana had two allies: her dad and money.

When Tawana was eight or nine, Junior began to let her count drug cash for him. Junior would later claim this never happened. "Don't believe everything she tells you," he says. Tawana, though, says she remembers putting bills into moneybags while he separated out some cash to shove her way. "This is for you," he'd say, and she'd take it. Ms. Jackson also kept Tawana supplied with money—legitimate money. She would give Tawana some at the beginning of the week and tell her to buy what she needed and budget the rest. But even with Junior and Ms. Jackson supporting her, Tawana wanted more. She began lying to everyone: "I needs this for school," or, "My granny can't afford to pay for this. Can you give it to me?" Then she would spend a little on school supplies and use the rest to buy drugs to sell, from which she would make more money, then buy larger amounts of drugs to sell, and make even more money. By adolescence, she was already in the game, and at fifteen, she had moved into her own place. Tawana, a.k.a. G. Wonna from Villains, had become a drug dealer.

Tink Tink, age six, spent the night before the takedown, June 25, 2003, at Tawana's house. Mimi and Big Head, his parents, had made Tawana, now twenty-two, Tink Tink's godmother. Tawana and Tink Tink were always together, and he preferred her in some ways to his own mother. Tawana bought him the things he wanted that his parents couldn't afford. Tawana would remind the boy that his mom was struggling and did the best she could for him, but Tink Tink was a precocious child. He knew, like Big Head had known, the rewards that dealing could bring even him. Unlike Ms. Jackson's place, the homes of Tink Tink's extended family members provided no refuge from drugs. Tink Tink was fourth generation in a drug-dealing family. Tawana never thought to shelter Tink Tink from what she was doing. He knew everything already, she said, and he wanted to know more. "What's this called?" he'd ask. "What's this cost?" She'd always tell him. She told him everything.

Tink Tink knew more about Tawana than most, and he had big ears. He even tried to warn Tawana about Crystal: "Girlfriend," he said. "I'm telling you, that lady work for the police." Tink Tink had heard it from his grandmother. He would say, "Watch, you going to go jail. You going to go to jail."

Tawana would say, "I ain't going to go to jail, you just be quiet."

She even had the boy with her when the feds recorded a damning wired transaction on April 9, 2003. Crystal got into Tawana's car to make the purchase, saw the boy, and tried to say, "Hi, Tink Tink, hi Tink Tink."

But Tink Tink responded, "Don't talk to me, because you're a police."

"Motherfucker, don't call me no fucking police!" Crystal shouted.

"You *is* the police. You probably got on a plug right now!"

"Shut up, Tink Tink," Tawana said. "You don't know what you're talking about."

Throughout the transaction, Tink Tink was firm. He kept saying to Tawana, "When you go to jail, just remember, I said it."

Tawana paid him little mind at the time, but when she arrived home Crystal's nervousness during the transaction bothered her.

> I'm all, "What you keep looking back for?"
> She like, "Nothing. I'm high, I'm just tweaked."
> So I'm like, "Okay."
> And after that, it was . . . I felt something. I just felt somebody watching me. And there was a white van across the street. But then I was like, nah, it can't be. It can't be. You know, I went to my Daddy. I told my Daddy, I said, "It was something wrong today. I think I . . . I think I really messed up today. It was something wrong. I didn't feel right serving her today." He like, "Don't worry about it. It's nothing, don't worry about it." So I left it alone.

The morning of June 26, Tink Tink was watching TV in Tawana's living room. He liked to get up early, around five o'clock, to watch cartoons. At six am, the police came to the door. Tink Tink ran to wake up Tawana: "Police at the door!" Eventually, at the direction of the officers, he went out onto the porch to wait for Mimi with his blanket and a pillow hastily stuffed full of cash that he later gave to Ms. Jackson. He watched as they clipped the cuffs on Tawana for transport to MDC downtown. They didn't hurt her, him, or anything in the house. They were polite.

Tawana had no idea what was going on, even after they told her that she had caught a federal case and was going downtown. In the staging area, she suddenly saw everyone she knew: kin, friends, acquaintances. Her mother, father, Big Head, Redd, Erick, Bengal, Black, Tina's boyfriend K-Rok, and a bunch of Pueblos were there. Her uncle Clifford had been targeted as well. A community writ small. Tawana thought of Tink Tink and his prediction. Her lawyer would later ask her, "Why didn't you listen to that little boy?"

Roughly the same experience occurred in separate locations all over town on the morning of June 26. People tried to contact one another in frantic early-morning phone calls. The police knocked on Ms. Jackson's door looking for Clifford. She let them in. "He's not here," she said, "but feel free to look."

And look they did. They told Ms. Jackson they would call her when they were through searching Tina's place so she could secure the door. Some police were respectful; others were not. People told stories of officers throwing residents against walls, mistaking kids for adults, and leading out at gunpoint people of all ages in their underwear. One of Juan Lococo's sisters, not yet three months' pregnant, began to have severe cramps, but the police would not bring her a chair until her mom threatened, "I don't care if you are the FBI, if she loses this baby, I'll sue your asses up and down!"[1] Someone brought her a chair.

Three days earlier, on June 20, Judge Paul Game had approved Special Agent King's request for twelve arrest warrants: John Edwards, Juan Lococo, Charlotte Jackson, Tawana Edwards, Brian Favors (Redd), Dante Washington (Big Head), Thomas Carl Adams (Woo), Erick Kennedy, Lincoln Widmore (Bengal), Kevin Allen (K-Rok), Emerson Silva, and Linda Bayer (Black). All were wanted "for violations of 21 U.S.C. §§ 841 (a) (1) and 846: possession with intent to distribute and distribution of cocaine and cocaine, base, and conspiracy to do the same."[2] In addition to setting up key probation and parole searches, King requested search warrants for eleven locations associated with those individuals: Junior's apartment, Tina's apartment and Ms. Jackson's house, Tawana's apartment, Juan Lococo's house, Redd's place, Big Head's, the Kennedy house, Bengal's distribution location (his girlfriend's house), K-Rok's unit in the projects, and Black's house. Four additional federal targets had separate conspiracy charges. The remaining Operation Fly Trap targets would instead face state charges.

King and Brooks had initially planned to call the task force Operation Charlotte's Web after the intricate network that surrounded Tina Fly, but a lawyer warned that the FBI might run into copyright problems with E. B. White's estate or Disney over the children's story that had inspired the name. So they settled on "Fly Trap" and kept to the FBI tradition of designating strategic domestic work with heavily symbolic militarized nomenclature.

Multijurisdictional task forces like Fly Trap had gained popularity in the years before 2003, and their deployment has gone hand in hand with new efforts to share information across jurisdictional lines. In departments as stretched as the LAPD, federal involvement was a way to gain funding for specific gang and drug eradication efforts. For a city the size of Los Angeles, its police force is tiny. Officers are sometimes stranded in emergencies, with backup too far away to arrive in a timely manner. L.A.'s infamous sprawl, combined with gang members' reputation for opening fire on officers, makes the idea of walking the beat laughable. Police recognize that, if limited to individual arrests, they will never gain any headway when it comes to gangs. Federal involvement brings money and manpower, training and expertise, and, perhaps most important, the well-honed practice of head starting broad-scale investigations with a U.S. attorney. Combining these federal tactics with detailed local knowledge of the players and streets makes task forces into antigang powerhouses.

Special Agent King met with variable reactions on his arrival in L.A. It took some cops a bit of time to get used to him, he says. The LAPD, with its renowned insularity, was not an easy friend to feds, who have also conducted internal affairs investigations into police wrongdoing. Officer Brooks was different. He knew what federal involvement could bring, and he intentionally sought out King as a federal partner—just one of several such collaborations in which Brooks would be involved in the coming years.

During Fly Trap, Brooks, King, and the other task force officers constructed their version of Charlotte's Web, establishing connections backed by supporting evidence. John Edwards, Juan Lococo, and Tina Fly were at the top of a classic bulletin board; their street servers and members of other conspiracies were featured below. By the day of the takedown, the FBI press office had morphed the task force bulletin board into a widely broadcast collective mug sheet—photographs with names, alternate identities, and a bright red "in custody" band across the face of each apprehended individual.[3] Department heads stood next to these images, which the FBI had blown up to the proportions of a Publishers Clearing House check, to have their own celebratory pictures taken. Their press conferences were covered by National Public Radio, the *Los Angeles Times*, and local radio and television newscasts.

ARRESTS MADE IN JOINT OPERATION FLY TRAP TARGETING VIOLENT LOS ANGELES STREET GANGS—Ronald L. Iden, Assistant Director in Charge of the FBI in Los Angeles, Chief William Bratton, Los Angeles Police Department and Sheriff Lee Baca, Los Angeles County Sheriff's Department, announced today the multiple arrests of various members of rival street gangs. Members of the Blood Stone Villains and the Pueblo Bishops were taken into custody this morning on various federal and state charges related to a criminal enterprise investigation of these two violent street gangs based in Los Angeles.[4]

In what he says was one of the highlights of his career, King was in charge of mobilizing over three hundred officers to capture twenty-eight members of the Villains and Pueblos. Officer Brooks would later term the takedown an excision: "We surgically removed those people," he said.

Brooks's statement, the Fly Trap publicity, and the many law enforcement documents supporting Fly Trap as a police action constitute a "narrative of precision." This narrative narrows public vision to the moments where intention successfully meets target.[5] Narratives of precision censor parts of a story, strategically remove individuals from certain social contexts, emphasize those same individuals within other contexts, and subsequently manufacture key images that justify the shape of police action. These images stand in contrast to the narratives that family and community members construct, which I term "disordering narratives." Disordering narratives disrupt the precision of the previous statement, bringing back mitigating factors such as poverty, employment, family, and other aspects of the story that go unheard or unheeded in court and media accounts. Precision narratives are the public claim, the distilled moment. Disordering narratives are usually more private than public. In Fly Trap, disordering narratives describe the toll of actions, a toll that reaches behind the list of targets. Names and images link to kinship, relationships, personal histories, and other untidy categories. Disordering narratives explode the Fly Trap mug sheet into multiple, jagged dimensions.

Peace officers are master wordsmiths in the narrative of precision; a just-the-facts-ma'am style of accounting has long been part of police procedure. This narrative's symbolic foundation in Operation Fly Trap represents a cleansing of poison (gangs, drug dealers, violent individuals) from the community and its "good" (churchgoing, decent, hardworking) members. Community members echo this divide at the same time that they disrupt the purity of these categories.[6] Narratives of precision, whether visual, written, or oral, can be as specific as they are erroneous. But theirs is always a truth claim, rooted in morality, that attempts to manufacture clearly defined kinds and categories.

Disordering narratives meld police action and criminal life firmly back into family fallout and community consequence. They counter decontextualized images by instead representing the voices of those outside of the power grid of mainstream life.

In the next few pages, I present three precision and disordering narratives to draw attention to the ways that they are equally constructed. None are explicitly truthful; they address different things for different reasons.

In the first example, one narrative represents the perspective of target Ben Kapone, the other the perspective of a law enforcement officer. The first, I gleaned from a law enforcement report the prosecution submitted to the court as evidence. I obtained the second account during an interview with Ben. Ben intended his narrative to summarize for me what happened the day of the sweep. It took me almost two years to realize I possessed two nonexclusive narratives of the same conversation.

Narrative 1 (law enforcement): S/Clemmons agreed to speak to me without an attorney present. S/Clemmons told me during the month of May he was the only person selling narcotics (rock cocaine, marijuana) from his residence ([address]). S/Clemmons told me he sells narcotics for pocket change and that no one else is involved in any type of criminal activity at his residence. S/Clemmons told me he is currently on parole for a weapons violation and is willing to admit in court that he has been involved in the selling of narcotics.[7]

Narrative 2 (target): They tellin' me that they been watchin' me, doing some surveillance for a certain amount of time. They got me doing some transaction with a person, they tellin' me all kinds of different kind of things. They like, "You know you a three-striker woo-woo-woop." I'm like "Yeah?" "So, we lettin' you know that's what you're charged for, with such-and-such, and you willin' to talk to us?" I'm like, "Man, I don't know what to talk to you about. If you saying that you got all this, what is there to talk to you about?" "Well, you gonna let your wife go down?" I'm like, "Go down for what? What she do? What do you got her here for?" It's like, "Well she's here because of child endangerment, because of the gun. We can charge her, charge you, then your baby would be alone left at home. They gonna put your baby in a foster home." I'm like, "Man, c'mon man, that's bullshit." One of the officers is like, "Ok, well you have anything to talk to me about?" I'm like, "I don't have anything, what is there to talk to you about?" "Well, do you sell dope?" I'm like, "Man I don't sell no dope; I got a job." He was trying to force me into telling him that I sell drugs at my momma house.

Narrative 2 is a blow-by-blow oral account of a conversation that occurred shortly after arrest, obtained as research, from the point of view of the arrestee, a former gang member. Narrative 1 is an after-the-fact written account of the same conversation, submitted as evidence, from the perspective of a law enforcement officer, a sworn affiant. The second narrative relates the not-so-subtle pressures and power plays that accompany attempts to solicit and avoid the admission of a crime. The first narrative is full of tidy statements, each cut, trimmed, and tailor-made for a court of law: that S/Clemmons agreed to speak without an attorney present; that he said he was the only one selling crack at his residence (his momma house); that he sold narcotics (crack cocaine, marijuana) for pocket change; that he was on parole for a weapons violation; that he was willing to admit in court he had been involved in the selling of narcotics. The weapons violation was a particularly sloppy fabrication, as S/Clemmons was indeed on parole, but for something else entirely. The succinct aspect of this narrative masks the messiness of the original interaction and points to the impossibility of a straightforward admission of guilt in a culture trained for its opposite. Whereas the second narrative hints at a potential toll on the family (the implications of child endangerment, the placement of a child in foster care, etc.), the first account benevolently severs the family from the guilt of the target and indicates that no one else at the residence was involved in any kind of criminal activity.

Even where they stand opposite each other, the narratives agree on two things: first, a conversation took place. Second, this moment of face-to-face interaction is important enough to narratize, to make part of the record, to recount in telling and writing. Both narratives capture the rare moment of direct contact, where years' worth of surveillance attempts and failures, and efforts to see into two cultures zoned off to outside parties culminate in a brief conversation.

The unsaid between the two narratives recognizes first that S/Clemmons may very well have been dealing drugs out of his momma's house but that he would never willingly admit it. He probably would not use the term "pocket change" to justify his criminal wrongdoing. Left unsaid is the notion that, despite the officer's moral certitude, the officer himself may take immoral steps to prove what he personally feels he knows beyond a reasonable doubt. The unsaid recognizes that human strengths and foibles often connect the two sides of criminal cases into one uncomfortable package.[8]

Another example of opposing accounts involves a discrepancy between FBI paperwork and a family narrative involving John Lococo and five kilograms of powder cocaine. First is the FBI account, on form FD-302, written by Special Agent Jose N. Moreno. Next is the narrative of the same event from an interview conducted with Juan Lococo's mother, Eugenia. Once again, I only realized later that form FD-302 was nestled among the rest of the case's public paperwork that I had copied at the courthouse.

Narrative 1 (law enforcement): On 7/1/2003, Special Agents Alexander R. Arroyo and Jose N. Moreno met with ELENA SANTOS LOCOCO, date of birth [date], of [address], Los Angeles, California. During a search warrant executed at her residence on 06/26/2003, LOCOCO was provided with an FD-597, however the following items were inadvertently omitted. On 7/1/2003, another FD-597 was provided which listed the items that were seized on 6/26/2003.
  a). Five "bricks" (one kilogram each) and 2 bags of an off-white substance
  b). One (1) clear bag of an off-white powder substance
  c). Four (4) baggies of various loose rocks of an off-white powder substance.
  LOCOCO stated that she recalled the above items being taken, but refused to sign the FD-597 on the advise [sic] of her husband's lawyer. A copy of the FD-597 was left with LOCOCO.[9]

Narrative 2 (Target's mother Eugenia): Okay, because then afterwards, after they took everything they took, they came back the next day and told my daughter-in-law that they wanted her to sign a paper saying that they had taken the cocaine, and this and that, because they didn't put it on the list of everything they had taken. And when Gracie called me and I was asleep, and she was like "Mom, get up." She goes, "Cause the FBI is coming. They want Elena to sign a paper." So I woke up. I took a shower. I went back and I told Gracie, "Tell Elena that if they get there before I get there, tell her not to sign nothing." When I got here, they were already there, and they were talking to her that nothing was gonna happen to her, that they just needed her to sign. And I said, "No, she's not gonna sign nothing." I said, "She'll take it to her lawyer." And he so, he told me, "She has to sign the paper." I said, "She doesn't have to sign nothing. She has the right to have a lawyer. She has a lawyer. He has a lawyer. Anything, it goes to the lawyer. The lawyer says to sign it, she'll sign it, if not, no." I said, "Why didn't you get this signed with the date yesterday?" They said, "Oh, well, we forgot." I said, "You didn't forget to have her sign the other papers." I said, "How convenient that you forgot this part of it, huh?" And they just looked at me. I'll never forget it.

The first discrepancy between the two accounts is the date. According to the FBI document, the interaction took place on July 1, four days after the takedown. According to the family, the interaction happened the next day, which would have been June 27. In the first instance, the special agents stated that Elena remembered items a, b, and c (the off-white substance) being seized but indicated that she refused to sign the paperwork on the advice of counsel. In the second instance, the family went into collective motion upon finding that the FBI was coming to talk to them. No lawyer was present, only a mother-in-law who made her skepticism regarding the omissions clear.

Despite the vast space between the two accounts, the first is more credible in the legal arena simply because it has the ability to become part of a public statement. The special agent's report has a file number, a special form, and a formal presentation. In other words, it has a place, legally and spatially. The family narrative has no place, no form, no file. The first has the force of the FBI behind it rather than the assertions of irate, overprotective family members, or people facing prison time who might be prone to perpetuating self-serving falsehoods. The first statement is the one that finds its way into broader public view, while the second, generally speaking, is relegated to ephemeral circulation in the community.

For law enforcement, excising the backstory of a statement is simply part of procedure. Going into so much detail ("I woke up, I took a shower," or, "The mother-in-law was acting like a pain-in-the-ass bitch that day,") would not be acceptable to writers of professional reports. Precision narratives depend on such omissions. By bringing them back into view, disordering narratives both recontextualize and question the content, motive, and power behind their structure.

In this instance, authorities had photographed the five kilos on site. Lost was Lococo's copy of the original FD-597 report, which had detailed what was originally seized. It disappeared when Lococo was in court one day. He handed it to the judge for review, and it was never returned. He wrote a letter to the court requesting it back without results. Lococo's eventual plea agreement was not based on the five kilos. The five kilos did, however, make it into the press release issued by the U.S. Attorney's Office upon the sentencing of the main defendants: "At the time of his arrest in June 2003, Lococo was found with more than five kilograms of powder cocaine."[10]

Special Agent King had heard the family's side of this story, and according to him the entire thing was a paperwork problem. It was not that big of a deal, especially because of the photographs, and certainly not big enough to warrant the alarmist reaction on the part of the family. But for Juan Lococo, the five kilos became a symbol of injustice, which he wrote and thought about a great deal.

A third example of precision and disordering narratives concerns gang membership and the symbolic transformation of nonviolent drug offenders into violent gang members for the purposes of the court and media. This transformation turns Fly Trap from a regular drug war case into an antigang campaign critical to public safety. Narrative 1 is from Special Agent King's affidavit to Judge Paul Game in which King filed a complaint against the target subjects and requested warrants for their arrest. It is dated July 20, six days before the sweep. This document gives authorities permission to conduct the task force sweep. In the first document are two of thirteen assertions regarding the gang membership or affiliation of target subjects. In the second document, several interview "responses" disrupt the allegations of gang membership of two primary targets, John Edwards and Tina Fly. I did not solicit these responses to counter allegations of gang membership explicitly. The topic of allegations of gang membership emerged repeatedly in interviews I conducted with the targets and their families.

Narrative 1 (law enforcement): Gang Membership and/or Association of the Target Subjects. 13. Most of the Target Subjects of this investigation are members or associates of either the Pueblo Bishops gang or the Blood Stone Villains gang.

a. J. EDWARDS is an "OG" (Original Gangster, a term which refers to an older, respected member of a gang) of the Blood Stone Villains, according to CS-2. CS-2 stated that J. EDWARDS utilizes the "YG's" (Young Gangsters) to protect his drug business if he has problems, and still associated with known members of the Blood Stone Villains. CS-1 has also confirmed that J. EDWARDS is a member of the Blood Stone Villains.

b. JACKSON is an "OG" of the Blood Stone Villains. During several interviews conducted over the past few years by members of the LAPD anti-gang unit and other LAPD officers, JACKSON admitted membership in the gang. During one of the intercepted wiretap conversations, JACKSON referred to herself as the only "OG" at a Villain party which was thrown for WIDMORE the night before WIDMORE went to jail for approximately sixty days. In addition, I have recently observed JACKSON associating with known members of the Blood Stone Villains, in areas controlled by that gang. CS-1 and CS-2 have confirmed that JACKSON is a member of the Blood Stone Villains.[11]

Narrative 2 (targets, targets' community):

Tina Fly: I'm not a gang member, I never was. As far as me, I associate with them, you know, I grew up around them and everything. But I don't gangbang, I can go anywhere I want to go. And Junior? He isn't no gang member! I had no tattoos or nothing that I was a gang member.

John Edwards: I'm not a gang member.

Renee Richardson: See that where they keep going on constantly about that gangbanging. And see then that's where I disagree, because I knew my brother weren't no gang member. I mean, as far as growing up in that hood, he probably had a couple of them fights cause they came on that street. But as far as to go over there and be hollering some gang slurs or to be around them, my brother was just that not—he was just not that.

Edwards's family friend: He's not a gangbanger. He's not a gang leader. That man stayed down his momma house. He grew up over there. Just because you grow up over there don't mean that you one of them.

Tawana Edwards: Tina ain't no gang member. My daddy ain't no gang member. I was a gang member. I should know.

In this scenario, a concrete definition of gang membership is part of the message of precision: it either is or it isn't. The first assertion in the affidavit is incontestable in that most targets in Operation Fly Trap were indeed gang members. Most of the Fly Trap defendants would call themselves members; others would term them that as well. But immediately following this assertion are the two statements that Junior and Tina Fly are gang members. The subjects, their families, and friends all contest these statements. The disordering narratives stress the nuance of association, of past and present, and complicate the matter of is or isn't. In the first narrative,

King recounts how CS-1, CS-2, some wiretap evidence, and previous police interviews provide proof of gang membership among these two target subjects. Asserting that these two key individuals are not gang members corrupts that message. Nongang membership is not as clean, and mere association not as convincing. Association because someone grew up in an area is a subtle business with no clear line to draw. The passage of time is also a clear factor. Perhaps a person had been involved in the gang during adolescence but is clearly not involved now. Junior, for example, was referenced in press release materials as a "founding member of the Blood Stone Villains," but the Villains had been founded some years before John Edwards had come on the scene. From the inside, neither Tina Fly nor Junior had been active in gangs for years if they ever had been. Simply occupying the same area and associating with members of a gang in the past or present, using the YGs to protect a drug enterprise, or even calling oneself an OG does not necessarily constitute actual affiliation.

The lack of gang membership asserted in the second narrative joins a disordering narrative because it disrupts the founding principals of the case. In this instance, most of the low-level players were gang members. But the three main dealers, each of whom received the longest sentences of more than twenty years, were not.[12]

The precision narrative of Operation Fly was organized around gangs, despite the main targets' lack of overt gang membership. Because Justice Department involvement in the case, however, partially depended on establishing the gang membership or participation of the subjects, court documents constantly emphasize gang materials.

*   *   *

Officer Brooks was itching to arrest two particular people who really were gang members: Big Head, from Villains, and K-Rok, from Pueblos. Brooks seemed to want these two so much that other defendants in the case regarded them as part of his personal vendetta. From Brooks's perspective, it was no vendetta. Brooks viewed targets like Big Head or K-Rok as pieces to a bigger puzzle. Figuring out how the puzzle worked, and each individual's role within it, was one of the best parts of his job. They had done nothing to him personally, but they had continually skirted the law to do as they pleased. Most of what they pleased wasn't good. Big Head, for example, was a Villain shot caller. He had the power to tell the other, younger homies what to do and had long-term involvement in local drug dealing. As far as Brooks was concerned, Big Head needed to be removed from society, period.

Kevin Allen was different. Brooks had always maintained that Allen—K-Rok—was a shot caller for the Pueblos. K-Rok denied it. But K-Rok was more than just a regular gang member. He had turned hustler. When he had become a pimp in his early twenties, his focus turned to the money pimping could bring him. His Blood status was understood, but he seemed even more concerned with fancy clothes, nice cars, fast women. K-Rok's flagrant disregard for the law to feed these overblown materialistic impulses rankled Brooks.

K-Rok had spent part of his childhood watching Crystal, who had lived next door to him in the projects, become a crackhead. He had noted her daily routine and saw her dip into prostitution to feed her habit. He never liked to deal with her, he says, because she was "a nasty person." He doubts she remembers they were neighbors, but he did learn a great deal from her. Later, as a gang member and drug dealer, K-Rok had a strict moral code. He never dealt to kids or near a school, and he refused to serve pregnant women. No one under eighteen could sell drugs for or near him. He picked up the name "K-Rok" because of his "other side," he says. "A lot of people have met that person. That's a person you don't want to meet."

Before his arrest, K-Rok ran a mobile business called Kevin's Fine Articles and More, and people who wanted to emulate his lifestyle and fashion choices were his best customers. For example, Kevin wore only $3,000 pairs of shoes. Kevin's Fine Articles and More helped homies get their hands on such things. He replicated his sense of style for others well enough to turn a substantial profit. Pimping and dealing provided his primary cash flow, but he liked to run this side business—a quasi-legitimate enterprise—and it attracted attention that attracted more money. Rok drank Cristal champagne on Sunset Boulevard for his birthday.

K-Rok never stuck to one woman, and this propensity for juggling multiple partners eased his transition to career pimp. He began to work closely with Black and Tina in the early 1990s, during Tina's full-blown crack addiction. Until he met Tina, K-Rok had conducted business mainly in the projects he knew like his "own name." But the main girl he pimped there went to jail, and a mutual friend introduced Rok to Tina Fly. Tina would smoke up K-Rok's crack and then turn tricks on Central Avenue, Rok's new hustling spot, to make his money back. "We were a good team," he says, but Tina's addiction placed a limit on how much they could accomplish together. She vowed to get off drugs and eventually succeeded.

After Tina got clean, everyone was ready trust her with large amounts of work. K-Rok helped Tina move out of prostitution and into drug sales. Their eventual relationship seemed a foregone conclusion, but Tina and Black had long been involved too. This resulted in the infamous Operation Fly Trap love triangle. Black envied Tina's relationship with K-Rok, but K-Rok couldn't have cared less if the situation hadn't caused him occasional diplomatic headaches. The drama kept things interesting for him, however, and he'd always said he wasn't the one-woman type.

After his arrest, K-Rok wondered why the feds felt they could record the intricacies of this relationship when it had nothing to do with drugs. Had it been voyeurism? Sitting around listening to other people's sexual habits? He knew there were laws against that sort of thing.

Conspiracy cases like Fly Trap depend on personal connection. The parties in and around this love triangle comprised Conspiracy 2 in the court files. Conspiracy 2 named Allen (K-Rok), Lococo, Jackson, and L. Bayer (Black) as coconspirators, and Lococo filled the only non-love-interest role of supplier. The officers and special agents chuckled about the love triangle, as they did with many things in the case. As one officer said, "You mean you're not going to write about the love triangle? You *have* to write about the love triangle!" They were grateful for something to lighten the daily grind of listening and watching. But they hadn't made the recordings for laughs or to scratch their voyeuristic itches. Love here was court worthy; it was definitely relevant.

A more familial love framed the rest of the case as well. Family ties and the trust that goes with them facilitate enterprises like the ones the FBI and LAPD attempted to dismantle among the Villains and Pueblos.

Operation Fly Trap was, if nothing else, a family story. From the core familial triad of Tina, Junior, and Tawana emerged a host of interconnections among the twenty-eight targets: mothers, fathers, baby mammas, baby daddies, brothers, sisters, uncles, children, grandparents, people who used to date each other, people who were best friends. "He has a kid by my cousin." Or "She's my auntie's best friend." Or "She has a kid by my sister's boyfriend."

The ties of long-term friendship and family extended inside and outside criminality, and bound targets and nontargets alike. These were not crime families in the Mafia sense, but they were families that, because of the severity of disenfranchisement in their lives and neighborhoods, were oriented around criminal activity to varying degrees. For example,

Junior and Tina had a long-term relationship and one child together, Tawana.

Tawana's sister, Joanna, was related to Big Head through her biological father.

Clifford Jackson, sought on state charges, was Tina's brother and Tawana's uncle.

Tina and K-Rok were boyfriend and girlfriend; Black and Tina were friends and love interests; so were Black and K-Rok.

Crystal's (CS-1) boyfriend had a child by one of Junior's sisters.

Emerson Silva had once had a crush on Joanna, Tina's other daughter.

William Reagan and James Reagan, both federal targets, were brothers.

Big Head (federal) and Nee-Nee Washington (state) were first cousins.

Big Head's aunt was James Reagan's wife's sister.

James and William Reagan were uncles to Nee-Nee and kin by marriage to Big Head.

Tawana was Big Head's son Tink Tink's godmother.

Tawana, Big Head, Redd, and Erick, all federal targets, grew up together on 56th Street.

Nee-Nee Washington and federal target Erick Kennedy were first cousins.

Big Head's sister dated Erick Kennedy.

Big Head and Brian Favors (Redd) were close friends.

State target Ben Kapone's wife was close friends with Erick Kennedy's aunt.

Raoul Kent (Lucky) was state target Freddy Hughes's nephew.

Crystal had a relationship with Big Head's mother, used to live with James Reagan's family and babysit his kids and Lincoln Widmore, or Bengal, and had a relationship with onetime roommate Tina Fly.

Some of Juan Lococo's family was either complicit or participating in Lococo's drug business.

Leroy McAdams had been to jail with Erick Kennedy.

Relationships like these demonstrate how the arrests and related media coverage help to rewrite gang and kinship networks, just as they had already rewritten local networks in addressing both poverty and crime. The sweep targeted certain patterns of family life because family life and criminality in the neighborhoods ran parallel to each other. In this context, kinship ties became both a finding and a direction for the project.

Outsiders find it difficult to understand how context shifts what a family may deem acceptable. Most families shun violent crime and make distinctions between crimes that do not hurt people and crimes that do. For most, drug sales are in the first category. Drug proceeds are something that families can ease into based on their material wants and needs. According to Ben Kapone, dealing drugs as a young teen made it possible for him to help his single mother support her four children. He soon assumed an adultlike station in the family:

> You know, when you is a kid growing up in the ghettos, you're starvin'. Your mom got a little food in the house, but you're starvin'. Because you know just as well as I know that blacks are fashion. We like to be fashionable. So I consider myself starvin'. Fatman looked out for me. He used to give me runs. At fourteen years old, I got $1,000. That's a lot of money at that time. I'm buying cars, I'm doing my thing, I'm the man, all the little girls love me, all the bros love me, everything is straight. I'm looking out for my momma, my grandfather knowing I'm hustling. And he tellin' me, "Don't, woo, woo, woo. You out there hustling, you got all this money in your mattress. Put money in the house." So by me seeing the little smile on my momma face, knowing that her 'frigerator super full, knowing her rent paid for, so she can buy her a couple of outfits of whatever maybe. That made me feel good. That made me feel good, so therefore I continued to do it.

Familial acceptance of illegal income does not necessarily translate into the acceptance of other criminal behavior. Ben recounted to me a time when his mother and grandfather—both of whom knew about his drug involvement—prevented him from committing a serious crime:

> The day of the lift [robbery], I go in there, I go in there to go get dressed. I take off my clothes, let's do the job and shit, so I can get in, take off, you know what I mean. And my mama set me down to talk to me. She's like, "You been home [from detention] for two days, three days, you ain't sit down and talk me." . . . I'm like, "I'm on a mission, I got to take care of something." Well, she like, "Sit down." My grampa's like, "Why don't you sit down, I need to talk to you about something." And we sat up there and talked for about a hour. By me sitting there and talking to them about a hour, saved my life. Because they went in there to do the robbery, but three of the homies got carried away. They got the

fucking lady to take her shit off and were raping the lady. . . . I didn't go because my mama made me sit down and talk to her.

The rest of the people involved in the robbery would serve long prison sentences for what had become a brutal crime. Ben did not because his mother and his grandfather had the resolve to interrupt him. They accepted his drug money but drew a line when they feared a young member of their family would do serious harm to himself or others.

Another difficult thing for outsiders to understand is the way that drug and other illegal, or legal, money confuse necessity and what seems like unnecessary material desire. This is the concept of "starvin" that Ben introduced, what one author calls the "intersection of lack and desire."[13] The impulse to feed one's family seldom stands alone.

This the meaning of the "Fly" in "Tina Fly." Fly means being fashionable, looking good, on the edge of taste. In some sense, the Fly is part of what authorities cannot tolerate, and part of what was targeted in Operation Fly Trap.

Consumption is a manner of controlling what one can in the time that one has and in the place in which one lives—a car as opposed to a house, for example, or one's presentation of self rather than the look of the neighborhood. Consumption allows people to possess prestige where they sit. The fashion drives the effort to take social power back from a system that routinely denigrates one's participation within it. It is about transforming the ghetto from a site of pathology to a site of social power. Some people in the neighborhood succumb to the pressures of poverty in a manner that reflects that pathology, in a manner that others consider "dirty." These people sometimes fail to keep themselves clean; their children may wear ripped or filthy clothes or may have ill-fitting, worn shoes. Even if financial support is unstable, avoiding the stigma of being dirty in a poor neighborhood is critical for self-esteem, group reciprocity, and local participation. Although materialism and survival occasionally conflict with one another, financial support of one's family and the "fly" are similar forms of asserting power and creating stability.

Wearing expensive clothes, sharp shoes, and driving an extravagant car are qualitatively similar manners of controlling the ghetto's impact—a broken windows theory from within that targets individuals and selective networks as opposed to neighborhood space.

The people I interviewed for this project frequently framed materialism and taking care of family in the same narrative contexts. They seldom referenced one without immediately referring to the other. The following quotations demonstrate how people explained drug dealing and combined categories that might seem contradictory to members of the middle class:

> Tina Fly, on money as addiction: And making that fast money, I got addicted to it. It was an addiction. But then, I was helping my family. You know where I come from. I come from a poor family and, you know, I was trying to help my mama.

> Ben Kapone, explaining the contradiction: This is how a lot of blacks that's don't have no education or been raised in the streets or gangbangin', this is how they get they money to feed they family: they hustle. But just being the type of people we are. I guess we always looking for a thrill, a high, a sign we live by luxury. Fresh shoes, fresh shirt, clothes, T-shirt, super clean . . . and got $20 in they pocket. (chuckles) We materialistic. At the same time we junkies for this shit, for the fast lane, for the high life, for the 'Hey, here I am.' We fucked up peoples.

> K-Rok, on the "one-eyed demon": It's hard to stay focused when you hungry. It's hard to stay focused when you're looking at that one-eyed demon, the television, and you're seeing Cadillacs and Lincolns and people wearing this and people wearing that. And this is the upper echelon of American society. So you want to pattern yourself or emulate the images that you see. And it's taking too long to go to school and to get a education and the schools are not schools, and you not going to get a job anyway. Then look at the color of your skin. So it's disheartening. And so then you turn to what you can't do and what you can't make money off of and what you can feed your family off of, you know and then a lot, and in a lot of cases, when bills are due today, you don't have time to get a job today and pay the bills because you're not going to get paid for two weeks. And everything going to be cut off. Now you way behind. You understand what I'm saying? You got to go out there and you got to do something to take care of your household. And any man—white, black, Asian, African, Korean, whatever—any man, is not to watch his family starve. No matter what he got to do. Rob a bank, sell some dope, whatever. He not going to watch his family starve, he not going to watch them be hungry. And he not going to watch them be without the necessities of life. Not no man that I know.

> Tawana, on materialism and necessity: I like clothes, shoes, stuff like that. And I did it for the material things and to make sure that I have money and whoever else had money, and take care of whoever else and everybody.

Tawana's father, Junior, entered the drug trade for similar reasons. At sixteen, Edwards lived around the corner from Genia Jackson's place on Ash Street. He had just started dealing when Ms. Jackson met him. She didn't disavow him, she said, because she could see he was providing for his family. "That's what I can know of Junior," she says. "Whatever he did, he made sure his mother and his sisters had money from those joints." I asked Ms. Jackson to explain to an outsider why it would make sense for a mother to take in money that resulted from illegal doings. Ms. Jackson replied: "I would have took that money to support my family. I would have. I mean, didn't nobody turn down nothing, because everybody at the time really *needed*, you know what I mean? And that's what goes on—that's what most people get their money from, from somebody that's selling drugs." In Ms. Jackson's terms, understanding the tie between the drug trade and very real economic need is critical to comprehending how people grow toward a tacit or explicit acceptance of drug-based or other illegal monies.

Many drug dealers hold legitimate, working-class jobs in addition to dealing drugs, and one form of work supplements the other. Ms. Jackson herself had dipped into fraud—white-collar crime—on more than one occasion.[14] Youth in particular sometimes choose drug dealing to give their family economic stability. Unlike legitimate forms of employment, drug dealing is rooted in neighborhoods where people already live, requires little education, and can withstand the interruption of prison time and community reentry.

Crime spikes in the United States have long been related to deindustrialization. This basic economic lesson has become divorced from popular understandings of crime and violence.[15] A time lag masks the relationship between crime waves and deindustrialized economies. First, factories closed, and people became unemployed. Within a few years, families began to break down. Nonviolent crime, substance abuse, and domestic violence all rose. These processes can take six or seven years after factory closure. But the real problems don't begin until about fifteen years later with the generation of children, like John Edwards, and their subsequent generations, like Tawana, who were raised in the midst of the family and community fallout caused by deindustrialization. Children like Junior, who grew up in uncontrolled family struggle, increasingly turned in the 1980s to the drug trade and the streets to mitigate their inability to access traditional economic opportunities for their families. Some of these youth also began to participate in and be victim to growing numbers of homicides. Such youth became entrenched in the drug game as a main economic enterprise and, with little to take the game's place, passed it down to future generations.

The impact of deindustrialization and rising crime rates on communities also engenders another kind of fallout: the impact of crime suppression on people's lives. Although intended to decrease incidents of crime and violence, crime suppression tactics that increase incarceration rates cause many of the same disruptions that massive job loss caused thirty years before.

This disruption is particularly true of actions like Fly Trap that target collectivities, gangs, or drug conspiracies rather than individuals.[16] Operation Fly Trap's main impact on the community was that it removed many aspects of an extended family at once. This sort of action has even greater effect in an area where demographics have shrunk for African Americans, as they have in this part of Los Angeles.

The historically black Central Avenue area that encompasses part of the Pueblos and Villains neighborhoods is now overwhelmingly Latino. Black flight east toward the Inland Empire, northeast to the Lancaster/Palmdale area, or back to the southern United States means that most of the remaining black families in these neighborhoods know each other, and many are related to one another. With such demographics, isolation from crime or its punitive consequences is impossible. A collective sweep such as Operation Fly Trap simultaneously removes many people who together are part of a much broader supportive network, further weakening the community for its most dependent members.

Both Tawana and Tink Tink, for example, lost key members of their families on June 26. Tawana lost a mother, a father, and many friends and acquaintances in the sweep. Her uncle was also implicated but never arrested. She herself would be behind bars for the next five years. Tink Tink lost his father, his cousin, his godmother, his "play" uncle, as well as others he saw on a daily or weekly basis. Tawana, as a young adult of twenty-two, was old enough to accept responsibility for her actions and to understand the consequences associated with them, but Tink Tink, a child of six, could only harbor a sense of profound loss. At least four of the people with whom he was closest, who gave him affection and support, were gone overnight. The feds' list, then, was not only peopled by criminals. Invisible targets such as Tink Tink also occupied it, and these invisible targets bore the brunt of the collective incarceration.

"He just doesn't understand people," Tawana said to me after I'd told her about an interview I had conducted with Los Angeles County district attorney Steve Cooley. I realized, during my interview with this experienced prosecutor and head district attorney, the vastness of the divide I had intended to bridge with this research. The bridge could be symbolized by having people like Tawana and Steve Cooley begin to, in Tawana's words, understand one another. Cooley, however, seemed to scoff at the possibility of considering broader socioeconomic contexts such as deindustrialization or poverty as root causes of gangs or violent crime. He did cite school failure, but it was fourth on his list, after drug addiction and drug abuse, the family, and the glamorous attraction of gangs and crime. When I pressed him on the poverty issue, he said: "I think that there are plenty of good poor people out there who are not engaging in the horrible crime of drug trafficking and justifying it by 'making ends meet because we're poor.' I don't think that's any excuse. And I think it just breeds further self-destruction. . . . You want to get rid of one of the core causes, more suppression in terms of narcotics abuse, use and abuse. It's a contributing element."

Cooley recognized that law enforcement alone could not solve the entrenched gang problem. It needed to be a bigger struggle, he maintained. According to Cooley, families needed to stand firm and not tolerate gang behavior, period. Other resources—Junior ROTC, Explorer Scouts, school activities, local marching bands—could give kids' lives meaning. The East L.A. Parents Project, for example, was a multiagency collaborative effort to teach individuals the skills they needed to save their kids from the dangers of gangs and drugs. Cooley would have had a field day with the number of kin ties between Fly Trap targets. They proved exactly the point he was making that dysfunctional families have passed gang-related and other criminal activities from generation to generation as something to be emulated. "And it shouldn't be emulated," he said. "It should be condemned." He continued:

All society should be condemning the manifestations of this criminal, criminally oriented, subculture. And that will include the parents, uncles, aunts, doing their best to say, "you know what, that was not a good thing for me. After all, look at my rap sheet. Look at all the time I was away from my family in the joint. Look at all the time I did, you know, in drug rehab." Maybe I should encourage the next generation to do it a little differently. Rather than sort of make it something to aspire to. . . . Parents, are, through their acts, example, attitudes, are encouraging it. And they have themselves to blame when one of their youngsters ends up in prison for life without, because of his emulation, admiration and aspiration to be just like them.

I had come to the DA's office for the interview because of a statement
Cooley had made during a press conference regarding a Pomona sweep
similar to Fly Trap. He said that "gang crime could be prosecuted and
curtailed only with the help of the families of gang members." He added
that they were in a position to stop the violence before it started. "It goes
without saying that there's only so much we can do. If the families don't
help, they are the ones who are in a sense, aiding and abetting murders
in Los Angeles County." Cooley stood by the quote as it related to that
particular case and that particular gang, based on the evidence they had
seized and the arrests they had made. He also indicated that he thought
the statement was "accurate as it relates to other gangs from Los Angeles
County, the state and maybe even the nation."

The counterargument, though, is that constantly focusing suppression
efforts in neighborhoods interwoven with kin and community networks
would further weaken families and communities, and in so doing encourage the same sorts of criminal behaviors that the DA's office was attempting to fight.

> But I believe there's an attraction to [criminal behavior]. And one way to hope-
> fully reduce that attraction, is to have society in general sort of say, you know
> what, this is unacceptable. This is a subculture. And we're not going to glorify it
> and sing about it like a bunch of these rappers do. Make it sound like something
> romantic. Because at the end of the day, they're going to get their romance in
> the state prison. Assuming they live that long. That's not a very romantic end-
> ing either.

Crime and the drug trade are not the only things to have emerged from
deindustrialized urban settings—so too have the romanticized practices
that Cooley finds so troubling: the hustle, the pimped-out gangster style,
the rap lyrics, the glamour of drug trade money, K-Rok's ghetto fabulous.
But this type of romance is not so different from the romantic image of
family members who hope to deter youth by preaching about all they
have been through. "Look at my rap sheet, look how much time I spent
behind bars." The countless narratives that Cooley suggests in lieu of rap
lyrics also have the same effect: young people look up to those who have
been to jail, been shot or stabbed, and fought and survived. Such narratives turn the detriments of prison or bodily injury—or even the separation from family—into a system of prestige. Most broader social forces
in our society channel youth toward alternative forms of expression and

identity. The Junior ROTC is no significant counter to the tidal wave of influence in the direction of the streets. Family struggle and survival connect more realistically to the overblown practices of materialism or the exaggerated postures of rappers than at first seems the case.

*　*　*

"You kidding, right?" Tawana asked. "Tink Tink?" Ms. Jackson had just told her that her godson, the boy to whom she had been so close, had been hit by a car while crossing the street. He was gone. They had been apart for so long, Tawana could not wrap her head around his passing: "I didn't believe it at first. I was like, I don't think so. They play so much about serious stuff. After a couple of days, I thought about it, and I said yes it must be true." Tawana cried for days. The entire Fly Trap network—both behind bars and on the outs—went into collective mourning. Tink Tink, that bright child, had seemed beyond death.

Just as Junior had drawn Tawana into the drug trade through money counting, Tawana also was partly responsible for drawing Tink Tink into the same way of life. Tawana used to give him a choice: he could either stay in the house or he could go outside. But Tink Tink never wanted to go outside. He didn't want to go home to his mother. He wanted to sit in the house and ask Tawana about everything. She would tell him:

> This is what I do. Either you want to be here or you don't. You can go home with your mother, but this is, this is how I have to survive. You know what I mean? Even though he love me and like being with me, I always explain to him, I just can't stop what I'm doing, cause he's not my child. I can't. I gotta pay rent and bills so I need to take care of my business. But he know what I do. Sometimes I did used to feel bad for the things that—I used to feel bad, 'cause . . . I be saying, I need to make money because you like to spend money and this is how I have to take care of you, you know what I mean? 'Cause your Daddy don't get you what you want, your mama don't get you what you want. And that's the only thing I gotta do, is be your, be a mother to you and help you. This is how I gotta help you. I gotta sell drugs. And he was cool with it. And everybody else used to always say that I was good to him, even though he knew all my business.

Community and family—and whatever we deem good about those two concepts—have many strengths and an equal number of corruptions. The good father is only able to be a good father by being a drug dealer—by having his kid count his money. The churchgoing grandmother has a gambling problem. The hardworking mom accepts dirty money into her house because it helps to feed her family. The dedicated cop falsifies documents in order to prove what he knows in his heart to be true. Tawana includes a six-year-old in drug transactions because those same transactions are part of what it means for her to be good to him.

The behavior outsiders may deem "immoral" or "dysfunctional" is always justified by contexts removed from public view and consequently subject to outsider condemnation. Corruption and circumstance become one and the same. If taken in context, they relate directly to the flawed priorities, unpredictable changes, uneven movements, and radical disintegration of state systems within neighborhoods in poverty. These corruptions, which exist at every level of ghetto life from living it to enforcing it, are the ultimate counter to the narrative of precision.

One last narrative of precision exists very nearly at the level of fantasy, and it comes from within gang communities: it is the idea of living a calm life and escaping the neighborhood. Family has become a liability. Family members do not help you. You do not help them. You sap one another's strength. They compromise you when you're trying to do right; you put undue pressure on them when you fail. This fantasy of precision may be to live on one's own, to live in another part of town, to live quietly, self-sufficiently. But it turns out that this would involve forsaking the ties that ensure survival of any kind. Within the network of reciprocity needed to survive ghetto conditions are both the tangle of criminality and the damaging result of its suppression. This is one of the primary lessons of Charlotte's Web.

CHAPTER THREE

Broken Families

All John Edwards, Jr., and his six sisters remember are the shoes. Their father had come over once, around the Fourth of July, and took them all out to buy shoes. There were no birthdays, no Christmases, no Thanksgivings. This man was an alcoholic who didn't live far from them but who didn't do anything for them either. One sister observed that he "did nothing but give us life." They had a thousand memories of their mother—her sweetness, stability, dedication to them, the freedom and strength with which she nurtured them. She tried to give them everything she could but had few means to do so. They grew up crowded into a two-bedroom apartment, in which Junior found himself the only boy in a sea of women.

In high school, Junior had tried desperately to connect with his dad, looking for mentorship, guidance, maybe even love, but his father soon died. By that time, Junior had become for his sisters the father they all lacked. Junior had also become an excellent boxer and was an avid Muhammad Ali fan. The requisite sports training, and Junior's pugilism, had helped the boy to survive the streets without much familial backup. Drugs had surrounded him at every turn. "It was no peer pressure and no violence," he says. Instead, it was a realization that the drug trade presented the most expedient solution to his family's problems.

At eighteen, Junior was in love. Tina was his first "real girlfriend," he says. Though he messed around with multiple women, with Tina it was different. When Junior found out Tina was sleeping around, he began to "do things to her," he says, "out of jealousy." It got even more complicated after Tawana was born and Tina got pregnant by another man. "I thought by hitting her, I could always have her. But that was not the case. I think it made her worse. Tina was . . . woo, hoo. A violent individual. Very violent," he says. He and Tina parted company, though the second child, Joanna, still took his name.

In the early 1980s, everyone in the neighborhood was selling crack. After a friend introduced Junior to PCP, he began to sell it on the streets. He managed to save over $20,000. Although tempted by drug use that sometimes dipped into these profits, his love for money was greater than his love for a high. He soon transitioned from PCP to heroin and cocaine.

By 2000, his connection with Lococo provided a unique opportunity to supply drugs to the neighborhoods he knew so well. As he rose to a position of prominence in the local drug area, Junior was surprised at how people targeted him, how they robbed his house because he had money.

Even after he became involved in drug-related crime, the moral core of his existence revolved around what really mattered to him: his family and children. "I was to business thinking about the streets," he says, "but my children was always in my heart." Only after their needs were met would Junior indulge in purchasing expensive things. Many people depended on him. He had accepted responsibility for his mother, children, sisters, sister's children, many neighborhood children, the elderly woman out front who waited for him to bring her ice cream. Junior, who carried the memory of his own troubled dad, counted fathering as his most important job, even from behind bars. "My kids' program is me," he once wrote me.

In court, defense and prosecution painted two alternate pictures of Junior. The defense argued that his impoverished family life and the troubles attendant on growing up in the ghetto had pushed him into a life of crime. The prosecution argued that Junior had consciously chosen his life of crime and ought to be held responsible for that choice. John agrees with both arguments: "I didn't grow up saying I want to be like this person or that person. It was what I chose. I seen people dealing drugs and that's what I chose to do. The money was fine ... what I did, I'm suffering the consequences of now and my kids dearly miss me. What we or myself didn't realize is that, when we get arrested, it destroy our families."

Junior was the linchpin that had held his extended family together. According to one family member, he supported "not just his family, but other people's family. He'd come, he'd talk to you. He'd let you understand and realize the facts of the real—about your family. Your family is all you got." Junior kept the kids going to church and school. He went to PTA meetings, took everybody to the amusement park, hosted family picnics, and every week he had soul food Sunday at his house. Everyone would come, and he would bless them before they ate. "It would be like family, just cooking and having fun, everybody sit down and eat."

Junior had five young children, six older or grown children, and a host of other family members whom he supported at the time of his arrest. He never distinguished between which kids were "really" his—anyone in his family was in his family. With eleven biological children plus step-children, six sisters, their children, and a mother dependent on him, these family responsibilities took on monolithic proportions. The drug trade combined with Junior's energy for all of these individuals allowed him to fulfill these obligations with generosity. But the obligations eventually stretched generosity's limits: "I was tired of them anyway," he says of his children. "'Cause there was just too many of them. I was just out there.... I was just out there doing a whole lot of rolling."

Fights with Carina, mother of four of Junior's kids, never had to do with other men. They were all about drugs. The two had met because Carina, an addict, cooked Junior's dope for him. Carina began to steal from Junior. He refused to give her drugs, and she stole more. Then the babies started coming. The fights between Junior and Carina always ended in violence. "It's a weird situation to have to put your hands on someone you care for," Junior says. "I am truly sorry for the things I did toward Tina and Carina. They have accepted my apology."

Apology or not, children generally lack the capacity either to understand or to forgive abuse between parents. But Junior's children tend to fault their mothers, rather than their father, for these transgressions. "He was violent," Tawana says, "very violent," unknowingly echoing Junior's words about Tina. But their mothers were violent too. They were the ones on drugs, the ones on the streets, the ones who couldn't take care of them. When Junior raised a hand against his kids, it never lacked control the way it did when he raised a hand against some of the women in his life. In his kids' eyes, his love and consistency as a father trumped whatever frustration, anger, and violence his children witnessed.

Claudia, mother of two of John's youngest, loved children as much as Junior did. At the time of our interviews in 2005, Claudia lived with her mother and her four children, the younger two of whom belonged to Junior. She told me she had "wondered when they were going to send somebody." She said she had always wanted to tell someone what was happening. "Things are hard," she said. "This is hard." She had expected someone to care. She had expected "them" to send someone who would listen. After Junior's arrest, the family had to move, and the little money

Claudia received from welfare was not enough to get them through a month. Without a car, she had trouble exploring different housing or employment possibilities. She was so exhausted that some days she couldn't get out of bed. On top of that, her father was dying, and she would take the bus from the Jungles neighborhood near Baldwin Hills to the convalescent home in Beverly Hills to sit with him. Claudia never let her kids see her cry. She kept it all inside, for them and for Junior: "When he call, I don't try to get him upset by telling him, 'You know, we don't doin' this right, we can't . . .' I don't do that. I just tell him we okay and I just pray and just ask the Lord to help us."

Junior and Claudia met when she was in junior high. Her brother had recently been released from prison, and Junior was helping him adjust to the outside. Whenever he saw her, Junior told Claudia to stay in school. Claudia would try to avoid him and this advice, but it eventually sank in, she said. She had never learned to read or write very well, and was embarrassed that people might laugh at her and take advantage of her. Many years later, she and Junior had two children together, and he became "dad" to her two older children. He was the only one she could turn to for help with things she needed to do, with forms she needed to fill out. Even with Junior incarcerated, Claudia continued to rely on him to complete paperwork she didn't understand. Junior never made her feel embarrassed or ashamed. For that reason, she said, she never messed with anybody but him. He, in turn, never laid hands on her, and never laughed at her. With him gone, she had no one she could trust.

Before the arrest, Junior would be there in the morning for the kids, ready to go. He'd pass out snacks and breakfast. He'd make sure the four kids were washed up, that they took care of responsibilities before having fun. Even from prison, he'd call in the mornings and ask the same questions: "Did you do all of your homework?" "Are you dressed for school yet? Well, go get dressed."

After the arrest, one of Junior's sons, Kenny, did not want to visit his dad. Claudia knew it was because the boy was hurting, but Kenny, at ten, couldn't articulate that hurt. "He don't want to say, 'Well, mom, this hurt. I don't wanna go,' or, 'I don't wanna see my dad.'" Kenny knew only that he did not want to set foot in that prison. Kenny stopped wanting to go to school either, and his grades began to suffer; Kenny had always been great at school. His parents had taught him and the other kids not to fight in school and never to disrespect the teacher. They taught him that school was the most important thing. His mom had certificates praising Kenny for listening well and completing all his assignments. The next year he was to start junior high—a telling transition for many boys and girls that age. Claudia worried that, without their father's help, the kids would all be at a disadvantage. "Because I don't have it," she said.

> I have it to show them and help them, but not all like he had. And that's the biggest struggle. [Kenny] wants him to be here with him so he could go up to him and look up to him and you know, tell him the problem instead of me. And you know, they be wondering—it's hard for them. It's just they gonna need that extra help, so, we just—every night I pray for them; ask the Lord to keep them safe, to help them to learn to be somebody big where they can go out and get them a job and be somebody.

For children, time is a fluid entity. A week can seem like a month, a month like a year. The lengths of prison sentences make little sense to them; they only sense the person's absence. Junior's children wrote letters to the judge asking him to send their father home. His daughter Jackie called Junior's lawyer on the phone to ask if he could bring her dad home. "I'll try," he said. Junior was facing life in prison.

In court, Louis Yablonsky, longtime gang expert and psychologist, defended Junior's parenting. Yablonsky has interviewed over 5,000 criminals and authored a book about fathers and sons.[1] Most criminals, he said, are "terrible fathers," but John Edwards, Jr., stood out as an exception. His involvement in crime stemmed from his environment and family responsibilities, not from any kind of psychopathology. Edwards was not beyond redemption, Yablonsky said. Furthermore, his younger five children clearly needed him. Yablonsky recommended that the court take Junior's exceptional fathering into account during sentencing. Junior eventually accepted a plea but received the longest of the Fly Trap sentences: twenty-seven years.

The twenty-seven years contrasted sharply with Junior's words to his children: "I'll be home in a minute." "Minutes" are the constant refrain of prisoners to their loved ones. A minute is the length of any prison sentence, long or short. "They don't understand the time," Claudia said of her children. "They don't have no idea of what this means. I tell them twenty-seven years, but they don't understand twenty-seven years. They just think it's probably a month."

After Junior's arrest and sentencing, the kids were inconsolable. Claudia tried to comfort them but would cry herself. "The police don't understand," she says. "The FBI, they don't care about none of that. They just want the person in jail, and they want it for a long time. My babies don't understand that."

Across town, Junior's sister Renee cared for two of Junior's other children—his youngest daughters by Carina, Nina and Carla. Just before Fly Trap, Renee and Junior had fought to get them out of foster care. Carina had since entered treatment for her drug addiction, but Renee had won the right to have the children in the interim. At Renee's, the girls regained the semblance of a normal family life. To her credit, Carina eventually beat her drug habit. But after Carina got the girls back, they would cry for Renee, and the eldest began to have problems in school. "She just seems so sad," the school counselor had said. As often happens in families, embarrassment or jealousy or resentment push people to sever ties. Carina cut Renee off from the kids for over a year, and the latter had to fight to see them. She couldn't talk about the children without crying.

"Wherever they was staying," she says, "they blocked the phone number out. And we were not able to call there no more." Renee was sickened to hear the counselor tell her about Nina's despondency, since she had "always had so much spirit."

Junior, who had been providing support for the girls, could no longer do so from prison. Renee found herself in a family network that was failing, compounded by a power struggle with the girls' mother.

*   *   *

The U.S. attorneys and law enforcement officers in the case assert that people like John Edwards harm their loved ones by drawing police attention to the family. Junior had eleven children by five different women, and he let one of them, Tawana, deal drugs for him. The U.S. attorneys knew of his abuse of Tina. They maintained that Junior's children were his victims, not victims of the system.

In 2000, *United States v. Aguirre* had allowed a downward departure from the sentencing guidelines in "extraordinary family circumstances."[2] For the defense in *United States v. Edwards*, however, this argument was ultimately unsuccessful. Even if it had been successful, such a downward departure would have meant shaving off only seven years from Junior's sentence. For his youngest five children, all of whom were under the age of ten, a decrease from twenty-seven to twenty years would have made little difference.

Because family dissolution trends prompted this research, I initially had constructed a survey aimed at every Operation Fly Trap target. Of twenty-eight people, seven responded.[3] In the wake of covert police activity, hesitance seemed natural. The surveys I did receive, however, helped me narrow the book's focus to the central families in Fly Trap.

The seven surveys corroborate studies of familial and community devastation conducted by Marc Mauer (*Invisible Punishment*), Nell Berenstein (*All Alone in the World*), Donald Braman (*Doing Time on the Outside*), and Jeremy Travis and Michelle Waul (*Prisoners Once Removed*). The families of Fly Trap targets dealt with financial difficulties, loss of emotional support from loved ones, and stress-related health problems (six of seven respondents). Four of those surveyed lost legitimate jobs; two of seven respondents reported the job loss of a person who was not a target. Three of seven families were evicted or had to change residence. Although only two of seven either had children who went into the foster care system or had family members who were arrested, three of seven targets reported that their children had experienced significant changes in caretaking conditions.

The most vulnerable in society—children, the infirm, and the elderly—suffer disproportionate damage from shifts in family circumstances. The children in Fly Trap suffered ulcers, depression, and failure in school, and many resented the police. State target Ben Kapone's twelve-year-old brother, for example, was so angry after the morning raid that he would flip off the police whenever he saw them (a dangerous practice for any young black boy). John Lococo's young niece sobbed hysterically while describing her uncle's arrest three years earlier. Several children refused, like Kenny, to see their fathers. When Tink Tink died, the entire Fly Trap network mourned and resolidified a kin community that already linked the prisons and the streets. The boy's father (Big Head), auntie (Nee-Nee Washington), godmother (Tawana), two uncles (James and Keith Reagan), and a play uncle (Brian Favors, Big Head's best friend) had all been among the targets and were incarcerated with others who had watched him grow up.[4]

Health complications became the most significant unanticipated finding of this research. Most treatments of health issues and incarceration tend to revolve around prisoners themselves. They deal with the crumbling health-care structures of prison medical facilities (particularly a problem in California) or the impact of elderly prisoners on prison system costs.[5] In all the families I interviewed, people had experienced health problems that ranged from mild to severe. Family members suffered from psoriasis, weight loss, chronic headaches, high blood pressure, and heart trouble, and three women had died from apparently stress-related causes. Ben's mother Linda had required hospitalization for her heart the morning of the raid; John Lococo's sister Marilyn and John Edwards's mother went into the hospital shortly after learning the length of prison sentences; Tina's mother, sister, and several others required hospitalization between these key moments. Most of these individuals were already in poor health: the weight of their situations coupled with the traumatic events surrounding the task force pushed their bodies beyond what they could tolerate.

The extended family network Junior had so carefully nurtured unraveled after the takedown. His mother had to move. Several of his sisters wouldn't speak to each other or Junior. Young relatives crashed in his mother's new living situation without permission. The financial support Junior had always provided vanished overnight. Ms. Edwards only attended one of Junior's court hearings. She went with Ms. Jackson, Tina's mom, and cried throughout the entire proceeding. According to one of Ms. Edwards's daughters, "She went one time and she saw her son shackled, handcuffed. They let him walk down out past his mother, past my mom, and he said, 'Mom, I love you,' and she start crying. And after that, she say she didn't want to see that anymore."

Junior had been his mother's primary emotional and financial support. When the family unraveled, Junior's ability to ensure that his mother was well cared for also disappeared. His arrest forced the rest of the family to restructure their lives in relation to one another, and the most senior member of their family suffered as a result.

Ms. Edwards developed such severe psoriasis in 2004 that pus oozed from her body. Like the high blood pressure from which she also suffered, psoriasis could have been a direct indicator of stress. After she knew Junior had been sentenced, she repeatedly asked, "When is he coming home? When is Daddy coming home?" Eventually Renee got tired of lying to her mother. For Ms. Edwards, twenty-seven years was unimaginable, a death sentence. Claudia says Ms. Edwards knew she would not live long enough to see her son again.

> And then it was hard on his mom 'cause his mom was missing him. I think that was why she kinda got sick too because she used to ask me every time I call like, "Um, do you think my son come?"
>
> I say, "Yeah, he's coming."

"Well a lot of people say he not gonna come."

I said, "No, he'll be home, he'll be home."

And she just got sick, 'cause she was in good condition. And you know when you can go visit your parents, take your mom oranges or apples or sit on the porch with her and talk to her—they miss that kind of stuff. So that was a big, big part taken from her that she didn't never see her son. So she was starting to get sick, worried, and just wondering when they gonna let him come home? And she passed away before he can come.

According to Renee, their mother "died from unhappiness." At the time of her death, she had been due to move back in with Renee:

> I was taking care of her, but she wasn't sick. I would just feed her and make her take her medicine. But she knew to take her medicine—you know she wasn't totally sick. I would just take her to her doctor and her dentist appointments, take her to lunch, just to be there with her, to get her away from the crowd that she was in. And then she died from unhappiness.

One day, Ms. Edwards got all dressed up and then she lost control of her bowels. The family called the paramedics, but she died in the hospital later that day. The coroner's report indicated that she died of natural causes. Renee says: "She knew she was going. When I told Junior that, he said, 'Oh, Sis, she knew she was leaving.' He said she knew. And then, when I told him, he said, 'I already knew it was coming.'" John wrote, "My precious mother was taking care of one of my daughter, and God call her home. My mother don't have no more pain, suffering, tears, no more nothing."

Understanding how Ms. Edwards's death relates to Operation Fly Trap requires understanding how people physically embody stress and disorder in their lives. This means looking to social rather than individual factors that contribute to illness. In other words, we must switch the gaze away from flawed individual bodies or psyches and onto the structures of society. Social context acquires a special gravity since Ms. Edwards's illness and death, and the illnesses of other members of the Fly Trap targets' families, seem as influenced by external stressors as internal ones.

For vulnerable members of the targets' families, Operation Fly Trap had an effect similar to that of a natural disaster. Relocation, financial instability, the stress of police and court proceedings, and the removal of key family members all contributed to the exacerbation of preexisting health problems among the families of Fly Trap targets. While debates exist concerning the specific causes of chronic illness, inequality and stress stand out as primary factors for why inner city residents suffer from high blood pressure, heart problems, diabetes, and obesity. Reactions to the stress of organized police action, courtroom unknowns, and the reality of sentencing point to similarities between these and the way people internalize other kinds of trauma.

The second critical factor contributing to the deaths of Ms. Edwards and two other women in this project is not ghetto-specific: it is the loss of key individuals in the lives of those who depend on them. For certain family members—particularly those in ill health—lengthy incarceration of a loved one can be likened to the permanent loss of death. This is especially true in the federal system, which routinely hands down sentences over twenty years. Among the three main families whose members each received such sentences, people talked about their incarcerated relatives in the past tense, as if delivering eulogies. Equating lengthy incarceration and death links the removal of key individuals with death and illness, among people in whose lives they played important roles. Both John Edwards and Juan Lococo fit such scenarios, and their absence impacted the most vulnerable in their families.

Lococo's mother Eugenia had seen trouble before the raid in June 2003. As a result of husband Angel's legal problems, court appearances, and jail stint, Eugenia had become severely depressed and took disability leave. The state doctor, however, declared her fit to work after four months—a diagnosis with which her own doctor disagreed—and she subsequently lost her job of fourteen years in January 2003. Still unable to work, she also discovered she was ineligible for unemployment benefits. When Eugenia lost her job, John met her mortgage payments and medical and living expenses. When John was arrested, the family had to figure out how to live without him. Eugenia became more depressed and attempted suicide out of a sense of responsibility for John's situation. She had to be hospitalized periodically after the sweep due to the many illnesses that plagued her in addition to the depression. The family's problems only began with Eugenia. The family said that, without John's positive discipline, his youngest sister began to use crystal meth. Lococo's wife left for Mexico with their two young children, and his youngest son developed an ulcer. John was placed in a federal prison fairly close to Los Angeles in Victorville but his sentence was indeed lengthy: twenty-two years. After his sentencing, John's twelve-year-old son refused to see him. Lococo's wife Elena left him, and Lococo himself said, "I may be able to be a father to my children from in here, but the one thing I can't be is a good husband." Elena decided to return with her two girls to Nayarít, the small town in Mexico where she was from, but found herself unable to get her old job back, which she had held for ten years before her marriage. It was the only employment opportunity in her town. Her kids needed things she could no longer afford to provide—clothes, shoes, lunches for school. Word also got back to L.A. that the same family member who had molested Elena when she was a child was now molesting John's three-year-old daughter.

John's sister Marilyn had just turned thirty-eight at the time of the sweep. She had four children and lived in the front house of the property, while John and his family lived in the back. John sometimes made her house payment. Marilyn, in turn, fussed over John like a mother hen. It wasn't an exactly equal relationship: John had the money, and Marilyn the disability. She was so obese that at the time of the sweep, she couldn't leave her bed.

Marilyn worried about John in prison. She would tell him, "John, be good. Please, John, be good. Take care of yourself. Be good. I don't want anything to happen to you." John's sister Gracie says Marilyn took the three-year period between John's trial and sentencing particularly hard.

> I guess she didn't think and I didn't think it was gonna be all that long. I said, "Well, maybe ten years," you know. Ten years will go by quick. I was even thinking maybe five years. But when my brother started telling me, "No, well they're probably gonna give me twelve," I'm like, "Twelve! That's too much." And he's like, "Well, maybe twelve." But when they started with twenty-two, I said, "What?" I'm like, "That's too much!" So when they told her, she got really sick.

The family at first tried to withhold the information about the length of the sentence, but Marilyn had known John's sentencing date. She told her sister, "You come and you tell me what happened. I know he's been sentenced so you guys just need to tell me how long is he's gonna be there." Marilyn had clung to the hope that they would let John out. The day her sister told her that he got twenty-two years, Marilyn sobbed for hours. Soon after, she became seriously ill. In the hospital, Marilyn cried to her mother about John's absence and her inability to visit him or wait until his release. One day, she couldn't move and died soon after.

Marilyn's loss, as with the death of Ms. Edwards, was clearly caused by compounding factors. Research on life in the inner city demonstrates that stress is a main cause of the preexisting conditions from which most women in this case suffered. As with Marilyn's emotional attachment to John, dependency on a key individual resulted in a breaking point—how not just police action but court decisions and sentencing got "under her skin."

At least one other mother of a Fly Trap target died shortly after the arrests. I cannot include her story here because of the family's hesitance to participate, but this woman's preexisting condition rendered her unable to survive without her son. She died while he was in court.

Women carry most of the family restructuring responsibilities after a disaster.[6] Like disaster, incarceration causes overnight change. Unlike disaster, the stigma and moral judgment surrounding illegality complicate subsequent changes. Outsiders often place responsibility for these crises squarely with families. As recounted in the previous chapter, most consider the family the cause of any problems or consequences related to illegality and imprisonment.

Outside forces, however, determine and sustain familial problems in the ghetto and draw these problems into the realm of policy rather than the realm of family or individual psychology. According to Loïc Wacquant, the problem of the ghetto as a whole "presents every outward sign of being *internally* driven (or 'ghetto-specific'), when in reality it is (over)determined and sustained *from the outside* by the brutal and uneven movement of withdrawal of the semi-welfare state."[7]

Incarceration accentuates the effects of the semi-welfare state in ghetto areas in a manner that particularly impacts women.[8] Prison sentences not only remove key individuals who may have become successful family members, but also place family members in the position of having to send money to the person who had been the primary financial provider. John Lococo says his family constantly has to provide for him. Like the other targets in Fly Trap, John found that his role shifted from providing for the family through drug dealing to forcing the women in his family, who had nearly nothing and few marketable skills, to receive collect phone calls and to send money constantly for his commissary purchases (food and clothing, soap, deodorant, shampoo, toothpaste, and toothbrushes).[9]

Critical financial support for a prisoner is often uneven because of its drain on the family. This unevenness creates tension between the prisoner and other family members as well as among the family members charged with supporting the prisoner. Other family members may have few resources available with which to help a prisoner. They may attempt to avoid involvement and further erode family networks through resentment or embarrassment. Ms. Jackson mentions other distracting problems: "We think about, oh, how we gonna do this and how we gonna do that, you know. If we have money to go do this or money to go on their books. We gotta choose between going up there to see them or making sure they have the things that they need." Limited resources force family members to choose between their own needs and the needs of the incarcerated. People like Ms. Jackson must internalize the stress of that responsibility to restructure the family.

The burdens on noncriminal individuals with incarcerated family members increase their likelihood of negative health, social, and economic outcomes; the cost to communities and the society they constitute is incalculable.[10] In a country with such high incarceration rates,[11] usually for nonviolent offenses, and in which one in every nine black males between the ages of twenty and thirty-four is behind bars, the suffering of children and the elderly, and the dissolution of family and community in the wake of incarceration are not inevitable consequences. They are policy choices.

During one conversation, I mentioned to Ms. Jackson that Tina could have lessened her twenty-five-year sentence considerably if she had given the state information on other people. Ms. Jackson replied she was aware of that, but Tina had always said she would never snitch. Tina had said that she could handle the time, "'if you can just hold up.'"

Tina told me, "I can do whatever I need to, if you can just hold up." Those were the exact words that she told me. It wasn't easy for me to walk into that courtroom and listen to all those things. I'm not going to tell anyone that wasn't hard, because it was. But I was there every time, being strong for them. I can't even tell you how hard that was. But I was a mother. After that day in court with Tawana,[12] which I told you about, I come home and I just start screaming. Neighbors came running, "What's wrong with Ms. Jackson?" And they came and just sit with me that day. It made me feel better, because they were concerned. But it took a toll. You know, you were a strong person, but to a point. And I had to go again and again. You know more than they do, cause I never wanted to tell them. I don't want to upset them. It's hard enough to just try to do time without worrying about your mother.

Ms. Jackson had saved the emotional reaction from her courtroom experiences for the minute she walked through the front door of her house. She was able to share her pressures with her family on the outside, with her community, and with me, but never with her daughter and granddaughter. She says that one day she will tell them. But she plans to tell them when it's all over, maybe even when they're standing looking each other in the face.

For her part, Tina Fly knows her mother suffers. I said once in a conversation with Tina that, compared to several other mothers in the project, her mother was doing fine. "My mother is *not* fine," she said fiercely. Of course, she was right. Ms. Jackson was not fine. Overwhelming sadness had taken a physical and emotional toll on both Ms. Jackson and on Tina's sister, Carlotte. Ms. Jackson had lost weight, making her already slender frame seem emaciated. Carlotte had developed such severe migraine headaches that she required periodic hospitalization. But Tina's situation did not force them to undergo as radical a familial restructuring as that experienced by the families of the other main targets. Most of her mother's previous network and her job remained intact.

Tina's wayward past had oddly protected her family from the impact of her incarceration. Because of her history of drug addiction, prostitution, and mental illness, Tina had played a very different role in her family than had Lococo or Junior. She had not supported her immediate family emotionally or financially, and her sister and her mother had been happy to see Tina manage her own household.

The cohesiveness of the conspiracy case, and its implication of so many members of her community and family (especially Tawana), dismays Ms. Jackson. She and many other Fly Trap family members believe the targets would have benefited from strict but fairer measures that would have reintroduced the convicted back into the community instead of cutting them off from it completely. Despite Ms. Jackson's relatively "positive" situation, she suffered both bodily and emotionally, and was direct kin to no fewer than four Fly Trap targets.[13]

Ms. Jackson's financial burdens at the time of Tina's arrest extended far beyond Tina and Tawana. The community reciprocity often present in poor neighborhoods was alive and well, and not long after Tina was arrested, Ms. Jackson took into her home a severely mentally handicapped woman and her daughter, who had been conceived as the result of a rape. For Ms. Jackson to see a disabled woman and her teenaged daughter out on the street, in danger of being taken advantage of, was more than she said God would allow. The women lived in Ms. Jackson's house for two years until the daughter became so unruly Ms. Jackson had to kick them out. But she felt she had done as much as she could. At the same time that she supported this small family, Ms. Jackson also paid the remainder of the rent on Tina's vacant apartment. With the burden of feeding additional mouths, paying Tina's rent and ultimately finding a storage space for her things, and sending Tina and Tawana each $50 a month, she suffered significant financial hardship. Ms. Jackson realized that what she'd hoped for wouldn't happen: Tina could not come home.

As with many others in this case, people had no outlet to express their feelings about their family members' incarceration. Instead, Ms. Jackson, Renee, Eugenia, Claudia, and others felt penalized, unheard, and misunderstood. A "vast social silence" surrounds the families of the incarcerated.[14] The pressures on children of incarcerated parents have received attention as an unanticipated cost of the prison boom and have now become a federal funding priority. The same government that has waged a relentless war on drugs now realizes the disastrous familial and community results of that war.

Denise Johnston, executive director of the Center for Children of Incarcerated Parents in Los Angeles, says one of the reasons child-based interventions have failed is that they remain focused on the model of the nuclear family. While the linguistic categories of "baby mama" or "baby daddy" have been coined to adjust to new familial realities, policy has yet to catch up. Johnston asserts that, to be successful, policy efforts must take into account the more complex family and residential structures that comprise the realities of impoverished families. Current policy excludes fathers in particular—fathers like John Edwards or Juan Lococo—who often have children by more than one mother. This exclusion is not benign; it is rather part of a process that demonizes nontraditional families that are simply adapting to ongoing cycles of poverty and incarceration.

At first, a man's multiple children by different women seems a clear result of the hypermasculinity inherent in street culture. But serial monogamy can be a reasonable response to poverty and incarceration, both of which necessitate shorter-term, flexible relationships. New babies in such relationships cement common-law connections despite the presence of other children in the household. Men like John Edwards care for more children than they biologically father. Thus the void of men in places with high incarceration and death rates recasts these eventualities as reasonable if not sensible.[15]

The skewed gender ratio in the African American community is so pronounced that an entire microfield studies its causes and structural consequences for families.[16] In the Vernon-Central neighborhood where this project takes place, black women outnumber black men by three to one. The families in this chapter live in a country whose drug laws have jailed radically disproportionate numbers of African American men in a city whose gang wars have already claimed many lives. Here, nontraditional family structure is a predictable by-product of these distressed and violent circumstances. If moral judgment can be attached to serial monogamy, then let it also judge the policy choices that have helped to create and sustain such severely marginalized reproductive circumstances.

Suppression actions like Fly Trap that target problem collectivities create a more significant domino effect in tight-knit poor neighborhoods than do regular arrests. Men such as Juan Lococo or John Edwards are tied to multiple nuclear and extended families, all of whose members are impacted by collective incarceration. Apparently unaffiliated targets like Tawana, Big Head, or K-Rok unite many of the same individuals, young and old, and their overlapping responsibilities toward those individuals comprise multiple parts of a neighborhood's survival network.

The most basic response to the stories in this chapter is to pity the kids, the elderly, and the infirm but to argue that their plight cannot be helped. The absent person engaged in criminal acts. For this, no other punishment but prison will suffice. One consequence of this punishment is a life of suffering for convicts' children, the responsibility for which rests on the convicts' heads. The remorse people feel for their choices is too little, too late. The Fly Trap targets don't evade the consequences of their choices. The targets I interviewed universally framed it in regretful past tense. Tina Fly knows that "what we did was wrong and I'm paying the price for it." She prays that Tawana will "get through this and get back out there in society and do what's right." Tina had calculated the risks of the drug trade on the basis of her previous experiences in criminal justice, all of which occurred in the California state legal system. California's system required hard evidence, had no mandatory minimum sentencing laws, and would have landed Tina with a harsh but more manageable sentence of six to eight years rather than twenty-five.

The U.S. prison boom at the federal and state levels stretches far beyond the ostensible need to punish crime. Past and present factors, such as historical racism, deindustrialization, skewed sex ratios, nontraditional family structure, violence and incarceration rates, and crimes of economy are all intimately related. These overlapping realities eventually begin to look like social values. Outsiders easily blame flawed people and flawed choices instead of the flawed systems at their roots.

Five years after Fly Trap, John Edwards's family has reconsolidated. Carina now brings the girls to visit their aunt Renee. They talk over the telephone, and the girls are doing fine in school. John's sisters talk once again, visit each other's houses, and exchange gifts on holidays. After her father died, Claudia moved east to Rialto in search of a quieter lifestyle. Things have settled into a new reality. Junior is still involved with his children's lives but in a very different way.

Juan Lococo's mother left South Central Los Angeles, but his sister and her family still live in the heart of 38th Street. Lococo's son, now a teenager, still lives in Pomona with his mother, has begun writing to his father, and is hoping to attend college. With all of the children in Fly Trap, the ultimate impact of parental incarceration is still unknown.

The stories in this chapter represent a fraction of familial outcomes associated with Operation Fly Trap. When I described to Special Agent King the deaths of the women involved in this project, he said, "It's a tragedy. It may be part of the system that's broke."

Law enforcement officials, and the broader social narratives that are based on their values, engender a certain style of laying blame. If one shifts attention away from the criminal, however, and toward a child or a mother or an elderly person, a different story emerges. This new story requires a kind of action different from police action, a kind of justice different from criminal justice. If the criminal justice system weakens families and helps to cause the dissolution of supportive networks, then the criminal justice system also must be considered responsible for both arresting and creating crime in communities.

CHAPTER FOUR

Cutting the Head off the Snake

Kevin Allen and brother Elijah hadn't known "blood" to signify much in St. Louis, Missouri. They did know, however, how to slap, pat, sing, and chant to do the hambone. When they moved with their mother to L.A., the boys became novelties. Kids played with them just to hear them talk. Kevin and Elijah listened back. In their first neighborhood, everyone said "cuz" in the customary Crips manner. Once they'd moved to Pueblo del Rio, a new word was "like the lyrics to a song," Kevin says. "Blood, blood, blood." And while language certainly carried deep meaning in St. Louis, they had never before lived in a place where the wrong word could get you into such serious trouble. On one of their first days in the Pueblos, they saw a group of kids drag a boy off the bus at 55th Street and Holmes and beat him for saying "cuz" to a girl. They would see this scene repeated countless times. "It happened so much," Kevin says, "that in the beginning, you would feel for the person getting beat, but after a while you stop feeling for the victim and start rooting for the beater. I was desensitized from seeing so many beatings, and I decided I wanted to be part of the beat-down team."

Any attempt to discourage the boys from joining gangs only encouraged them. Stories their stepfather told of his janitorial work at local schools opened their eyes further to the geography of gangs—Pueblo Bishops, Blood Stone Villains, 20s Outlaws, 53 Avalons, 52 Broadways, 59 East Coast Crips—and the nicknames of key individuals—Stomper, Lonely Blood, Doc Dirt, Pueblo Steve, Too Hard, Dangerous Dan, Spud the Blood, Fat Man. These high-ranking Pueblos became Kevin's culture heroes. He wanted to earn their respect and move in their circles of power. His willingness to participate in violence protected him and ushered him in.

After Kevin won his first fight against a Crip, he had a reputation to preserve. The resulting power struggle played out regularly on the grounds of Edison Junior High at 64th and Hooper. "School was not a place of learning for me," he says. "It was more like a boot camp getting me ready for war." Kevin averaged three fights per week.

By age eleven, Kevin carried a .44 Magnum short barrel. Despite the danger, the drug trade and wars between gangs filled life with opportunities to fortify reputation and pocketbook. The neighborhood was still majority black, and any outsider was a target. Older gang members showed Kevin how to break into the box that regulated the traffic signal at 55th and Long Beach and turn the light permanently red. Kevin and the other homies would walk among the stopped cars and rob people. Police placed undercover units around the intersection to no avail. They finally removed the signal entirely. Even today, the corner of 55th and Long Beach, crosscut by four sets of railroad tracks, has only stop signs.

Every Friday, Kevin would fight at school. Even when he lost, being a victim to the collective violence of other neighborhoods elevated his status just as much as delivering the beating. The first time someone shot him, homies visited him from near and far: he had taken a bullet for the hood. When he took on a number of 59 East Coast Crips one day at Budlong Park, he fought until he blacked out. Everyone at school had a story to tell about him. Retaliation for that beating soon sent him to the emergency room with broken teeth, broken ribs, black eyes, and swelling in his brain. "I stayed in the hospital a couple of weeks taking different tests mostly on my head because it had swollen from all the stomping on it. I felt like a celebrity."

The big homies began to include Kevin in their operations. They robbed enemy gangs' crack houses, unsuspecting Mexicans' wallets, and naïve drivers. Between the dealing and robbing, Kevin came into large quantities of cash. He gave some to his mom, stashed some in his room, and used the rest to buy drugs to sell. More violence landed him in juvenile camp, and eventually in youth authority, where he became acquainted with an even broader gang geography.

Inside, old beefs transformed into friendships, and new opportunities arose for retaliation and alliance. Whereas outside Kevin had his gun, inside he had to rely on wits and fists only. He had always been slender— years later Ms. Jackson would refer to him as "that skinny boy from the projects"— so he carefully calculated his attacks to maximize the impact of his blows.

While Kevin was incarcerated, his mother moved to a new neighborhood where, once again, everyone said "cuz." He could not live there after his release. He was, and long had been, a hardcore Blood from the Five Duse Pueblo Bishops, and had taken the name Bishop K-Rok.

For K-Rok, as for many of his peers, gang membership was a process rather than a one-time choice. Sometimes people point to pivotal moments in their lives—times when paths diverged and they chose the wrong one. But rarely would such choices have made a difference. There would have been another football game, another lift. Being a frequent witness to violence had unwittingly laid the groundwork for subsequent participation in violence: emotional divorce from victimhood and empathetic reversal from victim to perpetrator. Another Pueblo told me that, for many young people, "tears of sadness become tears of anger and hate." Knowledge of gang geographies and power hierarchies gradually expanded, from home to the local boundaries at schools, and later to juvenile camps and prisons, to regional geographies and statewide gang politics. Key neighborhoods warred as much as key individuals who had become archenemies: K-Rok from 52 Pueblo Bishops against Bo from 59 East Coast Crips, as much as Pueblos against East Coast.

The Pueblo Bishops and Blood Stone Villains were close allies for years. "A lot of dudes would claim both," Kevin says. "For example, some Villains, if asked where they were from, would say 'Villain-Pueblo' and if a Pueblo was asked would say he was from 'Pueblo-Villain.'" The two gangs shared initials and combined their names, PBSV or BSVPB, to symbolize the strength of their alliance.

That camaraderie evaporated in the late 1990s. The shift had roots in local demographics, recent Los Angeles history, and neighborhood and prison politics. By the late 1990s, gangs had anchored new patterns of animosity and alliance in L.A. Some Bloods and Crips began to be unified, some Bloods groups sparked chronic internal warfare, and some black and Latino gangs began lethal cycles of conflict. Pueblos and Villains, the two Fly Trap neighborhoods, were now enemies. Pueblos and 38th Street, a Latino gang to the north, were also rivals. And the Villains and 38th Street embraced their mutual enmity with the Pueblos.

*   *   *

In the early morning, on August 6, 2001, Maria Isabel Villalvazo, or "Bibi," heard a volley of gunshots across the street from her house. She ran for her father, who had been sitting on the porch drinking a beer, but a single bullet to the heart killed her en route—one of nine AK-47 bullets that ranged into her house from the gun of Pueblo Bishop Gene Sanders. Sanders had fired at rival 38th Street gang members but eventually received a life sentence for Bibi's murder. Bibi—a wife, daughter, and mother devoted to her only child—was dead for no reason.

Chief Bernard Parks called the murder "the type of crime that can paralyze a community," and that might have proven true in Bibi's case. But the community rallied around her family. They were sick of violence claiming good people, neighbors killing neighbors, and kids they had known for years running around with guns shooting each other. Six days after Bibi's death, over two hundred residents, activists, police, and politicians attended a "Stop the Violence" vigil. They planted a coral tree in Bibi's honor at nearby Fred Roberts Park, a site of frequent gang violence. Bibi's husband, Ricardo, vowed to those gathered that something positive would result from her death. A lawyer in the Santa Monica firm where Bibi worked as a legal secretary set up a trust fund to enable Bibi's daughter to continue her education. According to her employer, Bibi had decided to have only one child to ensure she would have the resources to pay for college; the law firm now promised to assume that responsibility. Bibi's loss had propelled a community at risk of paralysis into action.[1]

LAPD officer Mark Brooks remembered Bibi's murder as "the straw that broke the camel's back" at Newton Division. Something had to give. The homicide rate had risen to twenty-four murders from fifteen in the same period in 2000.[2] The night before Bibi's death, a nineteen-year-old had been killed a few blocks away, and summer wasn't over yet. Bibi's death and the general rise in fatal violence led Brooks to seek out Special Agent Robert King that August to hammer out some kind of plan. Bibi's death propelled more than just the community into action; it helped produce the task force that would become Operation Fly Trap.

Brooks already knew a great deal about the streets and about the Pueblos and Villains. He had spent his early youth in a Crip neighborhood in Watts, California, and dimly remembered the 1965 civil unrest. The Watts riots prompted his single mother to seek out a more peaceful environment in nearby Compton to the south. But Compton was no paradise either, and Mark's older brother Michael joined the West Park Pirus, a Bloods gang. Michael was wounded by gunfire when Mark was ten. Mark's mother shielded her youngest from a bullet when some rival gang members later shot up their house. She was hit in the leg. Mark's fear and anger might have led him down the path toward revenge, but his mother curtailed that cycle: she sent Michael to his grandfather in Louisiana, and took young Mark straight to Texas. There, he attended high school and eventually joined the Marine Corps.

Mark boxed his way through the Corps. His skill landed him on the fast track to the 1984 Olympics, and his boxing future looked promising. His lieutenant, however, considered boxing a waste of Mark's time. He forced Mark out of the ring and into the MPs. To Mark's surprise, he liked it. He never turned back. After many years in the LAPD, he eventually became a senior lead officer in the area that encompasses the Pueblos, Villains, and 38th Street.

By the time Mark was the senior lead, incessant warfare between the three gangs had mythical roots that tended to change with the telling. Pueblos say that one night in the late 1990s, a drunk member of 38th Street wandered through the projects, claiming that Pueblo del Rio was part of 38th Street and their hood. One Pueblo took offense and murdered the 38th Street drunk. The response to this event by 38th Street, to come through the neighborhood shooting, began the cycle of revenge between the two neighborhoods that has continued for over a decade and would later claim Bibi Villalvazo's life.

All of these fights would have been squashed had the Mexican Mafia not declared war against blacks in the late 1990s. Their green light for these attacks destined the Pueblos and 38th Street for cyclical warfare.[3] Black–Latino gang violence would redefine the landscape of gang warfare in the ten-year period following Villalvazo's murder. But no Blood anticipated the dramatic Blood on Blood warfare. Bloods had known infighting, but the conflict had remained in check: grievances would go around once and then stop. Bloods had traditionally remained unified to withstand Crips, who greatly outnumbered them.[4] This meant that Bloods automatically counted other Bloods—even those unknown to them—as allies, whereas Crips fought among themselves. Most Bloods had not signed up to fight fellow members.

The necessity of alliance between the neighboring Pueblos and Villains had offset the two Bloods groups' long-standing animosity. John Edwards's sister Renee remembers coming home from school in the late 1970s to find the street trashed with ripped clothes and broken bottles from a street brawl between the two gangs. Infighting had never lasted long, nor had it regularly turned lethal. But as the structural constraints holding the two Bloods allies together loosened, their tension took a deadly form.

Many gang members compare the Blood on Blood violence to a civil war, with "more people getting killed than when we was on the streets fighting Crips." Each death reverberated through both communities.

A Villain named Do Dirty sparked the Villain–Pueblo war. Do Dirty had robbed another member of his Bloods-based prison gang; the man happened to be a Pueblo. When Do Dirty later ran into the man he'd robbed on the street, he shot first, but his gun misfired. The other members of the prison gang captured and held him until a broader group could decide what to do.

Supposedly, Do Dirty never wavered even as his captors clicked a gun in his face. Some said that people burned him with cigarettes and urinated on his body. Others said that each captor had a turn with the killing gun. Do Dirty was shot over twenty times. The logic of collective execution is not unfamiliar. To cross a prison gang usually brings death. A killer—like a prison gang member—set free almost certainly means that person will return to kill again. By that reasoning, Do Dirty had to go, and had to go brutally to make the point. Do Dirty's crime and its victim's retribution were resolved with street justice, and within the context of common prison gang membership. But Do Dirty was a Villain and his killers were Pueblos. Ultimately, these street gang affiliations and not prison gang politics were what pushed the two gangs into chronic warfare.

Bibi Villalvazo and Do Dirty were both murdered, but their deaths typify two aspects of gang warfare: Villalvazo's its randomness and Do Dirty's its cold-blooded intent to kill. Villalvazo was not Pueblo Sanders's target; nearly a dozen shooters rained pointed vengeance onto Do Dirty. Whereas Bibi's murder represents the ongoing cycle of violence, Do Dirty's represents its inception. Both the Pueblos–38th Street rivalry and the Pueblos–Villains rivalry were based on issues of respect and disrespect that culminated in cycles of vengeance, a "means of establishing order in escalating disorder."[5]

Operation Fly Trap both responded to and contributed to this disorder. Crime statistics surrounding Operation Fly Trap raise the question of its efficacy at decreasing gang violence. In figure 1, which shows data regarding gang crimes by month within Newton Division for 2003, Fly Trap precedes a division-wide spike in gang crime. The activities of two gangs among the roughly forty present in Newton Division's nine-square miles make it difficult to tell if the Fly Trap disruption was the cause of this rise. In 2003, Newton Division demonstrated higher rates of gang violence than other LAPD divisions; the area seemed determined to stand apart from citywide violence trends.

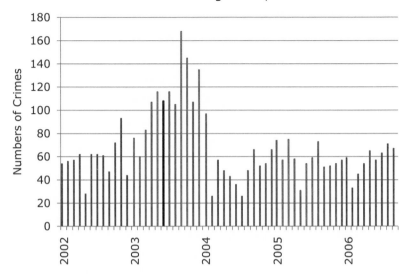

FIGURE I. Newton Division gang crime, 2002–6. Gang crime in Newton Division surged throughout 2003 and fell in January 2004. Operation Fly Trap in June 2003 is indicated with a dark line. *Source*: LAPD Online, "Crime Statistics by Month."

This upswing in violent crime returned to a more manageable number by February 2004. By all accounts, Newton police had seen a management crisis in 2003. After the arrival of a new, more effective lieutenant, the LAPD designated Newton as a pilot case for COMPSTAT policing. COMPSTAT combines statistical and spatial information to increase efficiency and accountability among rank-and-file officers as well as leaders. It was part of Bratton-era LAPD procedure.

By 2003, COMPSTAT had seen considerable success within police forces that had implemented it nationwide. Essentially a corporate model, COMPSTAT relies on sharing the computer-based statistics from which it derives its name. It creates more mentoring and accountability within police forces and prioritizes targeted crime data for happenings in a given area. The principles of COMPSTAT revolve around accuracy, intelligence, information sharing, marshaling of resources, in-depth analysis, rapid response, and relentless follow-up and assessment. According to the LAPD website, "the bottom line with COMPSTAT is results."[6]

The data in figure I indicate that COMPSTAT policing combined with the change in leadership at Newton Division—both implemented in January 2004—may have contributed to lower gang-related (and other types of) crime in the division within a short period. Although additional factors may have played a role, these two changes demonstrate that certain policing strategies and strong law enforcement leadership can make a difference.

Although Fly Trap did not impact gang crime in Newton Division as a whole, the task force did affect the two targeted neighborhoods. In the six months after the task force arrests, violent gang crime (homicide, rape, robbery, aggravated assault) among the Pueblo Bishops and Blood Stone Villains neighborhoods had declined by 37 percent (see fig. 2). Such a decline had been a goal of the sweep, and this one vindicated the law enforcement officials who had invested so much time in the case.

At second glance, however, the stasis of overall violent crime rates, including both gang and nongang crimes, counters the 37 percent reduction in gang violence. Overall rates of violent crime (homicide, rape, robbery, aggravated assault) in core neighborhood areas remained identical ($N = 78$) in the six months before and after the sweep. This means that nongang violence rose in equal measure to the decline in gang violence during the six months following the sweep.

Such a finding is not entirely unanticipated and can be explained in several ways. First, removing twenty-eight key individuals from an ongoing drug trade does not destroy that trade; it forces a shift in the players within a relatively short period of time. People don't stop dealing or using drugs because of surgical police action. Reconfiguring the flow of drugs could easily lead to violence in nongang arenas. Second, when undisturbed, gangs actually suppress a degree of violence because gangs control neighborhood violence as much as they proliferate it. Third, the targeting of gang leadership removes senior people, who exercise a measure of control over younger members, who frequently are more volatile. One fear is that, in the wake of an aggressive incarceration campaign that targets gang leadership, violence among the remaining, unrestrained members may actually rise. The sample size here is too small to prove anything definitive, but this increased variability between gang and nongang violence points to the destabilizing impact of the takedown at the community level.[7]

The impact of the takedown is strongest at the core of the two neighborhoods. The more broadly one construes the two neighborhoods' surrounding space, the less impact the sweep carries. If one extends the Villains' northern boundary to 48th Street, for example, violent gang crimes drop from 37 percent to 29 percent of the total. Gang violence declines further to 22 percent if the northern boundary is extended to include Vernon.

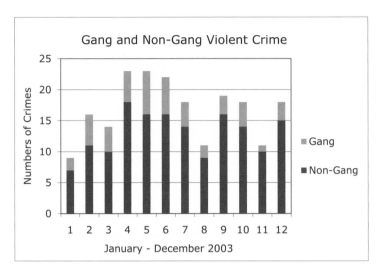

FIGURE 2. Gang and nongang violent crime. Violent gang crime in the Pueblo Bishops and Blood Stone Villains neighborhoods fell after the Fly Trap sweep (June 2003), whereas nongang violent crime rose in equal measure. *Source*: LAPD COMPSTAT records.

Narcotics sales and possession arrests rose slightly after the takedown, indicating that the task force had no effect on the drug trade itself. Dismantling the drug trade was not a stated task force goal. The task force used the drug trade to capture persons also assumed to be responsible for violent crimes.

Several flaws limit the interpretation of these data. First, gang-related crimes are generally underreported. To count a crime as gang related, police officers must have some evidence upon which to base that judgment.[8] Not all gang crimes involve someone shouting out a convenient gang name. People often fail to report violent crime as a whole. Particularly if crimes are between gangs, many assaults don't result in calls to police. Gang-related statistics, as one law enforcement officer told me, are a notoriously "gray area." People at all levels of law enforcement understand how problematic stats can be. The media quickly taps into exploitable imagery, even if the calculations behind them are as solid as possible. According to Sheriff Lee Baca,

Now what's interesting, sadly, about statistics. If you drop the crime rate at the same rate that it increases, it's only one-tenth statistically. Now, for example, if we end up with say 22 murders at the end of this year and then we jump back to the 68 the following year, it would be a 300 percent increase. But when you decrease it by the same amount that it increased, it's only a 70 percent decrease. So you're fighting a statistical battle going up that is three times as large as when you're going down. Your rewards are three times less statistically when you're going down. So I just look at statistics as being more of a problem than anything else.

Baca is aware that the public perceives the success of police work through statistics, and that both law enforcement and the media bolster their claims about violence through the use of statistics.[9]

The data presented here account for violent crimes only within the streets comprising the Pueblo Bishops and Blood Stone Villains neighborhoods. Crimes committed within those two neighborhoods by outside gang members are counted, whereas crimes committed beyond the bounds of the Pueblo Bishops and Blood Stone Villains neighborhoods by PB and BSV gang members are not. More precise analysis would require gathering data on crimes anywhere in the city that are associated with these specific gangs. Police simply do not chart crimes this way. In the central data-sharing offices, like COMPSTAT or the sheriff's department's LARGIN, no staff member prioritizes gathering data for such requests. Moreover, many gang crimes factor into ongoing investigations, about which officers simply cannot share information.

Despite these limitations, neighborhood-based data such as these remain the best indicators of task force success. The 37 percent decline in gang-related violent crimes and the rise in non-gang-related crimes imply the power of the task force to simultaneously decrease and foment neighborhood violence. In this particular case, the amount of rivalry between the two gangs, which localizes a degree of gang violence, supports this analysis.

The lack of comparative materials limits my ability to generalize this study's findings that the task force both increased and decreased violence. The analysis does demonstrate unequivocally the need to consider both gang and nongang violence when charting the impact of gang task forces or other suppression strategies. The paradoxical results in this case are predictable. One study, for example, showed that higher rates of incarceration also accompany higher rates of violence and that, when localities intentionally lower their incarceration rates, their rates of violence also decline. Another study showed that ramping up incarceration in a city one year creates a wave of violence the next.[10] The stress of punitive policing can raise the pitch of violence as well as lessening it.

Violence is a nuanced project among gangs. The exigencies of life shape the significance of gang murders and assaults. While the roles of victim and perpetrator seem opposed, their unity represents the core of what it means to be in a gang, where everyone is always both. Violence may be triggered by proximate causes (relationships, thefts, drugs, politics, insults). Midlevel factors include the drug trade and politics, broadly construed. (The Mexican Mafia's green light on black gangs is an example of a midlevel cause that combines both drugs and politics.) Ultimate causes of gang violence include state policies, economic contexts, and social inequality.

Gangs don't limit their death lists to those who died at the hands of enemies. Homies dead of heart attacks, car accidents, suicides, or police action are still dead homies. Among neighborhood killings, two Pueblo deaths in particular had a negative impact on police–community relations during the Fly Trap investigation. The first, that of Wolfe Lok, nearly caused a riot in the Pueblos neighborhood on February 18, 2003. Police maintain that Derek Jenkins, a.k.a. Wolfe Lok, had fired on officers first and had been on the losing end of a shootout that he initiated with police. The community conversely believed that the police shot and killed a man who was already down and no longer had his gun. Wolfe Lok had been under investigation and was suspected of a Villain's murder. When police happened upon Wolfe Lok in the projects, he supposedly began shooting at them. When police fired back and hit him, he went down on his knees and dropped his gun. As Wolfe began to get back up, they fired again and killed him.

By the time Mark Brooks's supervisor called him to assess the situation, Pueblos had massed on the streets. When an event like this occurred, Brooks knew, sometimes the wise stayed away to avoid further provocation. When Brooks managed to enter the projects, even those with whom he had a good relationship cursed him. One man threw oatmeal in his face. When Brooks came back hours later, Pueblos had knocked out a fire hydrant to wet the railroad tracks and draw police. They had blocked the Blue Line train with trash cans and sought out their allies, the Five Tray Gangster Crips, to fight alongside them. Brooks remembered: "And when I came down there, oh, my God. They were cussing me out. They had every gang member, everybody I knew out there. They were all angry toward me, like I did the killing. They all motherfuck . . . everybody motherfucked me. Everybody from the neighborhood that was a gang member yelled and screamed. And they all stood on the sidewalk and every one of them, everybody was like 'Fuck you Brooks! Fuck you Brooks!' Like trying to make a name for themselves."

Brooks knew why: Wolfe had been a Pueblo general. He was on their council, a neighborhood shot-caller, a shooter. Brooks was the most visible cop on the street and the senior lead officer for the Pueblos neighborhood. He made it his business to be in their business and was their self-described "arch enemy." Even on the best of days, people would call him a bitch or a liar. Whether this killing was just or unjust, Wolfe was one of two persons among the Fly Trap gangs killed that year by police action. These killings impacted an already shaky relationship between police and community members in Pueblo del Rio and contributed to the profound instability that accompanies untimely death of any kind.

During Brooks's first gun battle as a cop, he had killed a man. The drug dealer with whom Brooks had arranged a purchase had shot at some undercover officers and Brooks's return fire had been lethal. Brooks had also previously been shot while undercover in a Watts housing project. Unwritten LAPD policy allows wounded officers to select their next assignments, and Brooks chose Newton. In 1992, the year of the Los Angeles riots, Brooks arrived at Newton Division under the tutelage of an African American senior officer, who would become his mentor.

Brooks's frequent conflicts in the field made him a good judge of a situation, and he had been in more shootouts than the average cop. That day in the Pueblos, the situation had escalated into a full-blown standoff. Brooks assumed that most people were running off at the mouth, but their anger could have turned into something more serious. The homies were trying to incite some sort of action. A scrimmage line held gang members on one side, cops on the other, both screaming across the line. The LAPD positioned shooters on the rooftops and in helicopters, and suited up its riot police. And then Brooks saw William Reagan, who later became a Fly Trap target, behind the line of scrimmage.

"Hey, William," Brooks called. "Let me talk to you." Brooks considered William the only one there with common sense.

Reagan said angrily that Wolfe didn't even have a gun, that the police had just shot him down.

"Hey, that ain't what happened," Brooks said. He and some other officers explained what they had been briefed on early that morning.

Reagan vanished into the crowd and returned with a couple of Five Trays so they could hear it for themselves. After hearing the LAPD's side, the Five Trays withdrew their participation: if two armed parties had faced off, then Wolfe Lok's killing wasn't unjust. The Five Trays left, and soon Pueblo leaders heard the same information. Police began crowd-dispersal maneuvers, and Brooks directed the arrests of several people. The rest of the Pueblos disappeared into the projects.[11]

*   *   *

L.A. gang leadership structure depends on an ability to attract or hide itself at will from outsider attention. Independence and fluidity are nurtured responses to power incongruities. Some term this style of social structure "rhizomatic," "cellular," or "acephalous," meaning without a head.[12] In urban landscapes, nonhierarchical structure stems from arrests, forced relocation to prison, violence, and killing. The multiple segments of Los Angeles gangs fission and fuse according to local events, competition over resources (guns, drugs, etc.), migration, or outside influences (e.g., changes in crime policy). Flexibility and horizontal social structures resist suppression: a group's reliance on fluid hierarchy is a tremendous asset.

When police arrest what they assume to be gang leaders in Los Angeles, they often boast that they have "cut the head off the snake." Such assumptions reflect a misalignment between Los Angeles' and California's gang politics and policing styles based on East Coast gang archetypes. In Chicago and on the East Coast, gangs owe their corporate style of organization to the example of the Italian Mafia. L.A. has had no Mafia model—only a flat, decentered city in which to establish countless barrios and neighborhoods. Today, the main source of gang hierarchy is prison. The ability to move between prison and the streets cements the shape of this hierarchy while rendering the specific persons who occupy its positions of leadership eminently replaceable.

In L.A., punitive police action that targets specific individuals in order to dismantle an entire gang is flawed. Seeing gangs as segmentary groups means understanding the futility of searching for gang agency in conventional leadership or corporate-style organization—the two places law enforcement officials continue to seek it. Kinship, neighborhood identity, and political or physical location shifts define gang agency. Leadership does exist here, but it remains difficult to target and impossible to eradicate because others rise to take their predecessors' places. Ben Kapone once explained to me that Fly Trap's twenty-eight targets will give way to another twenty-eight, and to another twenty-eight after those. Thom Mrozek, a spokesman for the Central District of California's U.S. Attorney's Office, agrees: "We have cut the head off the snake, but the snake has a habit of growing a new head."[13]

At any moment, between five to seven people run the Pueblo Bishops neighborhood. They and their cadres function as quasi-independent cliques. Brooks says he needs to nurture an informant in each one of these subcircles to function effectively as an officer.

> The only way I get the inner details is when I got dirt on people.... Then the group will tell me more about what is really going on. And as a gang member you can't go up and just talk to people about what are you all doing over here and how you all doing, because they say, "What are you doing? Snitching?" So, I mean, for you to really investigate a group, you got to have different guys. Once you find out how the group functions, you go after different groups of different people. You also got to have more than one person within a group to verify that people ain't lying to you.

This is why, he said, Operation Fly Trap wasn't as good as it could have been. The two Pueblos who gave information only snitched on part of the gang, or not on their gang at all. Residents said the sweep missed some key individuals involved in the Pueblo's drug trade. Brooks had simply needed more information.

* * *

When Mitchell Gibson, a.k.a. Nutt, died, he wasn't even in the neighborhood and, unlike Wolfe, wasn't intentionally killed by police. His death nevertheless reverberated through the neighborhood as one more example of policing gone awry. The son of a Pueblo had passed away and most of the homies, including Nutt, were in attendance at the memorial service. Special Agent King, along with several other law enforcement officials, had received information that Nutt would attend the funeral at Inglewood Cemetery. They had Nutt under surveillance, and he was wanted for murder. The officers all agreed that, out of respect for the family, they would not disrupt the funeral to arrest Nutt but would wait until after he'd gotten into his car and left the cemetery to pull him over.

Nutt was riding with friends in the back seat of a rented PT Cruiser when the police maneuvered into position. Six marked cop cars surrounded the Cruiser, two in the back, two in the front, one on each side. The lieutenant authorized a single officer to do any shooting that became necessary, since this would minimize mistakes or accidents. After halting the car, King and the other officers got out with guns and told the people in the car to get out. Both the driver and the passenger got out and lay down on the ground. But Nutt had other plans.

The FBI already knew of Nutt's declaration that he never would go back to jail, so they were not entirely surprised when he jumped into the driver's seat and peeled out onto Manchester with police right behind him. As his car crossed Main Street, Nutt looked back to see if his pursuers had cleared it as well. He failed to see an eighteen-wheeler unloading gravel in the middle of the street. He crashed into the semi and died later at the hospital. King suspects Nutt had tried to provoke deadly force. He was waving his hands out the window, and officers thought he had a gun.

It is impossible to know whether dying in a blaze of glory was preferable to going back to prison for Nutt or Wolfe. Engaging in a shoot-out with police or embarking on a car chase demonstrates a fatalistic philosophy sometimes called suicide by cop. Sheriff Baca says it puts multiple lives at risk:

> So you've got a situation where you've got a gun, you got a gang and you got a car. So let's just go out and put ourselves at risk. And then we've got this fatalistic philosophy that "I don't care if I live to be twenty years of age so let's just get on right now." There's no long-term thinking in these individuals' minds. So it's a real tough thing for police to have to deal with because it is a sociological problem that is of a magnitude that is much bigger and problematic than resources are available to solve.

Gang members know their risk of death is high; they accept that risk as part of what it means to be a gang member. Murders can involve innocent bystanders, but there is no such thing as a gang member who is in the wrong place at the wrong time. By doing things that harm other people, gang members accept that a bullet may take them some day. The bullet may be random, but they are not random targets.

Moral codes govern gang violence. A "pass," for example, allows an enemy to go free if he or she is with family or other innocents. Ben had once been targeted while his wife and children were with him and explained that he'd have accepted his fate had he been alone.

> You corner me by myself, and you gun at me, I'm going to accept it because I'm part of, I was part of this gang. But my kids in the car, my wife in the car, you could give me the pass. I gave dudes pass all the time, right, when I was in the gangbanging really tough. When I was out there on the streets doing my thug

business, you know what I mean? I was, I gave dudes pass. You with your kids, you with your mama, you with your wife or something like that, that's a pass on. And by yourself, probably be a different thing. I'll gun your ass down. But if with your kids, I won't do that, because they don't have nothing to do with it. And dude should have gave me a pass. All the rest of 'em gave me a pass. All of them told him, no, man, don't touch him, let him go. He's straight, man, he's straight. Young dude, trying to get a stripe, he know if he kill me, he going to get that stripe for himself. He going to be put up a notch. Then he going to climb ranks in his own neighborhood. I didn't mind him trying to get me. But to try that with my wife and kids, in front of my kids. He hurt them. It doesn't matter what he is, police, black, white, Mexican, anything. I'll take your life. God as my witness, I'll take your life. I'll come and get you. No matter what the consequences is, no matter what, if I go to jail for life or gunned down, whatever—I got to get you.

Not all gang members practice violence equally. Some keep their eyes on the paper—the money—and fuck the rest. They want to do business and not to hurt people. They consider it ridiculous for others to risk their lives for the sake of other people's money. They may call the shots, but with materialistic rather than violent goals. Others are the "enforcers"— they possess the respect that enables them to speak out at a gang meeting and the wherewithal to take action on their own if necessary. Shot callers can also order others to such ends. By contrast, those who never rise to any kind of notable power are "foot soldiers." Occasionally, foot soldiers get off on the violence. They want to punish and inflict suffering. They may be intelligent, but they lack discipline. Other gang members generally don't respect such people. Their fetish of violence makes them unpredictable, addicts to be shunned. But unacceptable behavior has its place: these same foot soldiers can get things done when necessary. Gratuitous violence—shameful, sick violence, even—serves a purpose within the broader framework of the gang, but most gang members don't practice it, can't relate to it, and even abhor it.[14]

Unlike foot soldiers, enforcers, and money guys, the few individuals at the top of gang hierarchies—true shot callers—are highly visible targets for both law enforcement and other gang members. They are aware that rivalry or politics, in the end, may take them down, and any individual's leadership may be contested or short-lived. Gangs, then, rely on leaders to order their worlds, but internally they impose a rotating egalitarianism through continual competition and replacement.

K-Rok described the fate of Pueblo Steve, who was a "BIG," or Blood general, and had made the initial decision in the late 1980s prohibiting nongang members from selling drugs in the projects. Gang members represented the hood in correctional facilities of all kinds. They ran with other Bloods, and their good name protected people from the hood while they were behind bars—whether or not those people were formally affiliated with the gang. They also kept the neighborhood safe from the economic intrusions of outsiders, and they regulated, questioned, and fought when necessary. Gang members bore the brunt of whatever violence accompanied the drug trade. As both victims and shooters, gang members were the focus of frequent gunfire and were also in charge of retaliation. With these reasons in mind, Pueblo Steve decided to implement exclusionary rights to the profits from dope dealing in the projects.

Pueblo Steve flat-out rejected the separation politics among prison-based Bloods. He ran the projects at a time when street Bloods' unity remained the order of the day. The division between two California prison gangs, Blood Line and United Bloods Nation, ran counter to Steve's belief that all Bloods should unite. He also knew that prison gangs would sap neighborhood strength. They would demand revenues from the illicit Pueblos' economy—revenues that Steve felt should have remained in the projects. And they would inevitably force people to kill their own homies. Pueblo Steve never caved to continual pressure to be "on the paperwork."

Steve had always counseled the young homies to remain "uncut." By avoiding prison politics, they would never be put in a position to kill members of their own gang.

> If the rank come down, if the call come down for me to kill my homie, I got to kill him or be killed. If you're not in politics, you ain't got to take part in that. I ain't got to kill none of my homeboys. I ain't got to do that, I ain't got to touch it. If I'm a Blood Line, protocol come down, the chain of command calls for me to take this person out—I'm either going to have to do it, or I'm going to have to face the consequences.

Before his death, Pueblo Steve had mentored many young homies in the neighborhood. He had showed them how to scheme, move in silence, and gather information through observation. He preached discipline and unity. Pueblo Steve was a Big Homie: he ran everything that went on in the Pueblos projects. In his case, politics intervened to take both his rank and his life. Someone in a yellow Cadillac coupe rolled up on a corner crowd that included Steve and opened fire. By the time the police arrived, Steve had died.

Many young Pueblos, including K-Rok, grew disillusioned after the murder of Pueblo Steve in 1992. Rok had been in that corner crowd and had watched Steve bleed to death. After Steve's murder, K-Rok grew more isolated. He began hanging around with drug addicts, prostitutes, and crack heads instead of his homies. K-Rok considered himself a money addict. He still supported his hood, but gangbanging no longer held the same attraction for him. He took the best parts of his life—his family, the girls, and the money—and he left the violence behind.

This change in K-Rok coincided with a major event, the 1992 L.A. riots. Nothing that unfolded surprised K-Rok—not the beatings, not the lying cops, not the verdicts—except that other gang members were thinking the same way he was. The birth of his first child at this time, coupled with Steve's murder, set the stage for his transformation, which fed into a city-wide decrease in gang warfare that had partly resulted from the riots.

> Violence begets violence, and only love can conquer hate, and only true for-giveness for transgressions against you can you begin to truly heal from within. It was a shock then a joy when two Crips in full gear came walking onto 54th Street where mostly all the Bloods from my hood hang. They announced that they were willing to lay down the gun for the cause of black unity if we were. I was all for it. Can you imagine all the gang members in L.A. standing as one voice for change? Bloods and Crips laying down arms against each other and arming ourselves with the goal of change and equality? I was on fire.

Although the peace that resulted from the riots was short-lived in some places, it was not short-lived in K-Rok. He supported local alliances; he attended a global peace summit in Geneva, Switzerland, with other neighborhood activists. Although pimping and the drug trade continued to be his financial mainstays, he never returned to the violent lifestyle he had honed as a young gang member.

K-Rok and Officer Brooks had known one another a long time. Brooks knew all about K-Rok's chosen profession but could never quite catch him at it. He did catch Rok with quantities of cash a few times, but the dice Rok always carried in his pocket provided an easy way out. K-Rok gambled; that was why he had the money.

Brooks didn't believe for a minute that Rok was into peace. Not for peace's sake, anyway. He was into peace for the profit of it, to benefit himself. K-Rok counters that he "was one of the main proponents of 'Stop the Violence.'"

> It didn't make no sense: "I grew up with a lot of you guys." When Tina went over to my neighborhood, she had no problems. Because people know she's there to visit me. Just by doing that, it has a domino affect. Someone is at my house, they don't bother her. Then another person has to respect that. One of my best friends is from Villain. He wasn't on nothing. He wasn't trying to hurt nobody, not trying to kill nobody. I'm not with the violence. You can't make no money with violence.

The fewer dead bodies you have, K-Rok says, the more money you can make.

> Funerals cost about $6,000. That's like a down payment on a business. Then you got to spend money on flowers, on the party after the funeral, on something to wear. By the end of it, you done spent close to $10,000 that you could have spent on something else. And think there might be four or six funerals during a year. Instead of putting money into a video store or a laundromat to further your business, you had to spend it on funerals.

K-Rok was the first to admit that Brooks was correct. He wanted the money.

Violence notoriously obstructs drug revenues. Many consider the drug trade a primary cause of violence, but the opposite is also true. Economist Steven Levitt and sociologist Sudhir Venkatesh conclude in their study of a Chicago gang's finances that gang wars "are costly, both in terms of lost lives and lost profits." [15] Almost all of the deaths of drug sellers are concentrated in war periods. Moreover, the violence keeps customers away. This negative shock to drug demand is associated with a fall of 20–30 percent in both the price and quantity of drugs sold during fighting, and the drug operation becomes far less profitable. Chicago and L.A. gangs and drug trades differ dramatically, so violence and nonviolence reverberate in unique ways. L.A. gang members consider that less violence will not only minimize funeral expenses but also curtail police attention on the gang. Prison gangs frequently attempt to enforce peace to maximize the smooth flow of operations, and street gang members expand the base of neighborhood alliances to maximize their profits.

Gang politics in the early 2000s provided plenty of opportunities for new association. The memory of the riots as well as traditional intergang alliance techniques gave shape to unification efforts that now included previously inviolate divisions between Bloods and Crips. Many people helped broker the partnerships that developed during this period. Some remembered friends from their old neighborhoods; others might have had family on another side of town whom they had never met because the gangs got in the way. When the Five Tray Avalon Gangster Crips joined the Five Duse Pueblo Bishops to fight the police after Wolfe Lok's death, for example, their alliance had already been well established. Just as Pueblos and Villains used to combine their names, so new coalitions necessitated new monikers. Avalon and Pueblo together became the Avalos. Extending further, the so-called Aloways connected Avalon, Pueblos, and the 52 Broadway Gangster Crips. These groups had picnics, and basketball and football games—all traditional gang alliance mechanisms. For some, these events meant peace, pure and simple. They meant leaving behind the chaos, the drama, the corpses. For others, peace also brought an opportunity to expand business. However short-lived, these new relationships were a win-win.

Keeping or expanding peace to enhance drug profits was the opposite of what happened during L.A.'s early crack trade. In South Central L.A., the arrival of crack in the 1980s encouraged the restructuring of old gangs and the genesis of new ones. Existing neighborhoods cemented their territories; new arrivals claimed the null space between existing neighborhoods. Crack and guns together made the period between the 1980s and the early 1990s one of the most violent in L.A. gang history.

By the time of Fly Trap, territories had already been locked in for some years, and a current of peace remained strong within the black community. Highly visible peacemakers worried that the police didn't distinguish between peacemakers and gang leaders: "Bringing gangs together to stop some violence to bring some peace in our own neighborhood—it affects the police. I don't understand it. Why should it affect you? Anything, it should be helping, it should be cooperating, that you ain't got to be scrapin', scrapin' and scrapin' another dead boy's body off the ground."

Police hold little faith in local peacemaking attempts and mistrust former gang members who turn into community activists. The chronic antagonism between police and gang peacemakers leads individuals to question the motives of the police in disrupting internal gang unification procedures or targeting leaders. Police trust neither because they view peace-maker motivations as ultimately anchored in illegal profit. Police thus scrutinize and sometimes penalize efforts that might bring some calm to chronically violent situations. Gang members and community members in turn consider that police do this to keep law enforcement numbers up, since gang violence helps keep police in business.

On its face, this argument holds little water in Los Angeles, which has one of the smallest police forces relative to the size of its population and geography. In a city of four million people, with 400 gangs and over 40,000 gang members, the LAPD has just under 10,000 sworn officers. In this per-petually stretched context, reframing gang violence likely provides relief for the existing police force, and as well as impacting the ability of the po-lice to request special grants or federal involvement that bring additional resources.

If Brooks holds that peacemaker K-Rok had an ulterior motive, K-Rok maintains that Brooks has one too. Brooks has always proclaimed an interest in the community. He used to go around the neighborhood gath-ering kids into a school bus. He would take them to the park to do activi-ties. All the while, K-Rok claims, Brooks would really be gathering infor-mation about neighborhood goings-on. He wanted to build trust—and future informants—through his good works.

Among gang members, Brooks has the reputation of being a bitch, a liar, a user, a power tripper, an asshole, and somebody who was mean for no reason. I heard all of these things said about him at one time or another, long before I ever met him in person. Graffiti on the wall the day after Wolfe was killed blamed Brooks for the incident, even though Brooks had been off that day: "BIP [Blood in Peace] Wolfe. Fuck Brooks," it read. The Fly Trap defendants universally hated Brooks. K-Rok said about him, "How could you work for a system that's basically here to lock your peoples up? That commit cultural genocide against your people? I never could wrap my mind around that." Brooks countered that K-Rok is the one committing cultural genocide. Drug dealing brings slow death to the black community of which they are both part:

> My conscience is totally the opposite. K-Rok was selling dope right across from the elementary school on Holmes. He don't care about anything but making money. In terms of black officers, there needs to be a balance. We need to be a reflection of the community we make up. Somebody's got to represent the com-munity. All I did was respond to what was going on down there. It was killing

and selling drugs. I been there, and I seen good people down there. I seen how gang members target good people. I see the victims. I see the aftereffects.

K-Rok in turn countered that

In order to change any system, you have to become a part of the system, to learn the rules in order to be able to change it. And he in a position to do that. And make it fair for everybody. But he don't want to do that. He want to do, for lack of a better term, what they tell him to do. And that's what he do. And believe it. And he really believe. You supposed to believe in what you doing but, not to the extent where you committing a racial genocide, you know what I'm saying?

I asked K-Rok why the racial genocide part was okay for him but not okay for Brooks. He responded, "It's not okay for either of us." Brooks said of K-Rok:

He's trying to say I'm whitewashed. But he can't wash the black off me. I'm trying to do my job. When I got transferred out of Newton, people wanted me back. They wanted me back down there, because I was keeping peace down there. I don't even pay attention to a comment like that. Nobody has to tell me that I'm black. He's trying to look at the whole picture, what he needs to look at are the decisions he made in life.

The two squared off one time, outside Kevin's uncle's house. The champion boxer versus the Crip-tested Blood. Neither seriously injured the other, and the pride of both remained intact. I often considered the similarities between the two men, though they would have hated the comparison. Both men were gregarious, smart, and funny. Both were great storytellers. Both were into power in their own ways. And both were men into strategy. They weighed the risks, measured their moves, and relied on wits, training, and experience for survival. There were differences, of course. Kevin was a lady's man, for example—his ability to juggle women was partly what had led him to pimping. Mark was strictly monogamous.

Mark and his wife had been married for twenty years. When Mark was shot in the field in 1991, she freaked out. She went down to the station and declared that Mark was no longer working there. Never again, she said. No more undercover work. Fly Trap was twelve years later.

If Brooks knew he was going to "get" these people someday, the Pueblos and Villains also knew that they had to get him. At some point during the Fly Trap investigation, they felt him getting too close. A council of senior gang members decided they had to do something about him—something permanent. Brooks only heard about the contract on his life after it had already been called off. The Pueblos involved had planned to kick in a radio call, wait for Brooks's squad car to show up, and hit him in the crossfire between two AK-47s. By this point, the Pueblos and Villains already knew a lot about Mark Brooks. They knew the hours he worked, his days off, and when he went on vacation. The one thing they didn't know might have saved him had gang leadership greenlighted the contract: as the senior lead officer, Mark didn't answer radio calls.

That kind of coincidence wasn't the only thing that safeguarded Mark. His childhood in gang neighborhoods, experience in the field, and familiarity with the area provided him with a constant blanket of protection.

> I trust my judgment. If I see something, and trust me, you know, I'm from the neighborhood. I can see something. When I look at the neighborhood, I can see things in the neighborhood that most people can't see. I can see when somebody's acting different. I spend all my time down there. I spend more time working than I do at home. I drive through the neighborhood, I'm able to tell you, turn a corner and I'll tell you everything you gonna see cause I done drove through it so much. And it's not the entire division, it's just that area. So, I can see things out of place.

At the time the hit was put out on Brooks, he had numerous sources in the neighborhood. One of them was a Pueblo named Thomas Carl Adams, or Big T. After his arrest some weeks earlier, Big T had begun working for the Fly Trap officers. He had agreed to wear a wire but wound up going sideways. Big T mistakenly thought he could give a little information and return to his old life. Even if he didn't help the cops the way they had wanted him to, however, he convinced the homies to call off the hit on Brooks. Somehow, this gamble didn't bring suspicion down on Big T. Brooks says the homies lacked the guts to go through with the hit anyway.

At the end of the unrest surrounding Wolfe Lok's death in February 2003, K-Rok made a quick getaway after Brooks singled him out to officers. A few days later, cops managed to detain K-Rok for obstruction of justice and resisting arrest. He was taken to jail, booked, and held without bail. There, they threatened him with everything they had: phone calls, pictures, videotaped surveillance, and informant information.

He was supposed to do what Crystal had been doing: wear a wire and conduct controlled buys. At first he agreed, but, like Big T, K-Rok "flipped out on them," Brooks says. He was supposed to have given them the structure of the gang, but he stopped calling. When police lost contact with K-Rok, they stopped considering him friendly, and he formally became a Fly Trap target.

> See, once we brief you, we interview you and you tell us what you know, what's going on, then we know about you. And that's how he became a target. I mean, he told me in jail, he told me, he said, "I screwed up. I was part of the A-team and I couldn't break that gang thing." So he became a target.

K-Rok had been the key to uncovering the Pueblos network. The task force considered Pueblos more violent and troublesome to the community than Villains, but Fly Trap arrested more Villains than Pueblos. K-Rok had refused to give information on his own homeboys.

> I had information on everyone—in both neighborhoods. I could have put every single person in my neighborhood under and walked away scot-free. But I stayed away from my neighborhood. I gave information on the Villains, but not on the Pueblos. I just wanted to do enough so I didn't get a life sentence, which they were trying to give me. I mean, I got a family. I like women. I like to sit out in the sun—free. I like to cook what I like, eat what I like, when I like—free. I don't like to wear beige *every day*. The hood not gonna love you like you love yourself. You got to save your own life.

K-Rok's and Big T's refusal to cooperate, Brooks says, prevented police from penetrating the core Pueblo group they had intended to eradicate.

> The Fly Trap ... I mean we got the people. But we wasn't able to really penetrate things like we should have. And I didn't know enough that the next ... because you know I did another investigation after that. And that's when I really got the knowledge of how to go at a gang.

Post–Fly Trap arrests and deaths among targets confirm the utility and futility of taking people off the streets. Thomas York, twenty years old at the time of the sweep, died in a gang altercation soon after being released. Ben Kapone, who served only three years for Fly Trap, struggled with drug addiction after his release and was killed in 2008. Lucky, a man from

Pueblos whose state charges did not stick, was arrested for murder after Fly Trap, as was Erick Kennedy from the Villains neighborhood. Many of those whose activities were confined to the drug world returned directly to their previous activities after serving their sentences.

Law enforcement officials believe these people would have benefited from serving more time. More time might have prevented the deaths of those who were murdered and the actions of those who committed the murders. More time, according to law enforcement, might also have given people a chance to learn a different way of life, one that doesn't involve drugs. At the very least, more prison time would have removed them from these situations for longer.

Looking back at the list five years later, Brooks identifies five of the twenty-eight Fly Trap targets as "violent"—enforcers or shooters. Fly Trap targets identify fewer. One of the identified violent individuals, for example, fights if necessary but doesn't shoot. Another has perpetrated violence but recently attempted to leave the gang life behind. Another was the girlfriend of a shooter who would store guns at her house. According to several defendants, none of the Fly Trap targets was responsible for the rampant violence in the neighborhoods at the time of the sweep.

Anonymous: It wasn't nobody in that circle with us. It was kids, minors. Brooks never ran into them. They always stayed out of his way. He don't know the head honchos, the head shooters. He think he know that, but he don't. There's people that's not even on our case that's shooters, that kill people. He think he know, but he doesn't know.

Tawana Edwards: No violence, just . . . there wasn't no violence. It was only drugs. That was it. No violence, no. Not even no guns. I mean, they tried to say that because that's what the Villains are known as, murderers, gang members, I mean stuff like that. But our case don't have nothing to do with weapons, no murders, no none of that. But they, they always, they always say like, you guys are killers and stuff like that, when we're not. All we do is sell drugs and that was it. As far as murder somebody, no. Maybe you were on the phone with someone who did. Maybe the Pueblos are. I mean, it may be other people that done stuff or whatever, but everybody on this case, mm-mm.

Tina Fly: We wasn't like the mob. Putting people in freezers and extorting people from they business. We about getting our money and raising our kids, but we not active. We did grow up, we once probably was. But as of right now, we far away from the gang thing. We about keeping the peace so we could get the money.

Operation Fly Trap targeted, prosecuted, and incarcerated key members of the local, gang-related drug trade. It effectively pursued people committing drug-related crimes and took them off the streets. If this indeed was its goal, then it did its job well. If, however, the task force had a broader goal—to attack gangs, the drug trade, and make a lasting difference in gang-entrenched communities—then the task force did very little.

Five years after Fly Trap, violent gang crime in the Pueblos' and Villains' neighborhoods fell slightly. Violent gang crimes, including homicide, aggravated assault, and robbery, averaged 3.4 incidents per month in 2008 as opposed to 3.8 incidents per month in 2003. Although a difference of 0.4 may seem small, it constitutes about a 10 percent reduction in violent gang crime, which indeed provided some relief from violence on the ground. This reduction, however, is not entirely a success. During this same period, nongang violence in the two neighborhoods fell by a far greater percentage—37 percent. Drops in gang crimes in all of Newton Division between 2003 and 2008 run roughly parallel, with a fall of 40 percent. What requires analysis, then, is the considerable disparity between the decline in gang and nongang violence within the two neighborhoods. The disparity suggests first that gangs in this area may have been resistant to law enforcement tactics successful elsewhere, and second that for some reason the Pueblos and Villains, and perhaps other gangs, have been able to progress independent of broader trends.

Today, the Pueblos and Villains have stopped shooting each other. In 2008, older members of the gangs reached an accord: don't mess with us, and we won't mess with you. Pueblos now have to make a left on Compton Avenue from 55th Street to avoid the Villains' neighborhood. And Villains can no longer go to the projects. The Pueblos have expanded their base of Crip friends to include most of the Eastside gangs in the 50s blocks: 52 Broadway Gangster Crips, 53 Avalons, and 52 Hoovers. Many Bloods no longer like the Pueblos because they are so heavily allied with Crips. While the Pueblos are in the process of shifting their loyalties to other gangs in the 50s, the Villains still try to play by the old rules. Despite the changing landscape of gang life in L.A., allegiance to colors still carries weight.

CHAPTER FIVE

The Prosecutor's Darling

Wilma Jones kept a folder full of letters written for Tina in her office at the House of Refuge. Tina had told her, "You take care of me, so that the way you get the whole check. I don't care how much it is." For now, it was $200 for the bed and two SSI checks a month. In return for this payment, Wilma would accompany Tina to court, craft occasional notes to the judge documenting that Tina was in a secure residential facility, and periodically verify that Tina had suffered a mental breakdown, was heavily sedated, and would be unable to attend court. Wilma had kept Tina out of jail for the duration of the year in which Tina had faced a state drug case. Tina paid her in return.

This time, they just had to figure out a date for the letter. The people at Kedren Community Health Center wouldn't give Tina letters if her main therapist was out of town or unavailable. Tina proposed that she and Wilma should simply take an old letter (the good one), change the date on it, photocopy it, and submit it. Wilma agreed.

Wilma laundered all of the money through the houses where she helped troubled women. Her employer, House of Refuge, was a reputable but underfunded residential treatment facility for a small number of drug-addicted women. Wilma had overcome her own drug problems and believed God had spared her to help others like Tina. Wilma tried to stay focused—for Tina and the other women in the houses—but occasionally she would seclude herself to break down.

When Wilma indicated she would not be able to attend court after all, this provoked both Tina's wrath and her self-admittance to the Augustus F. Hawkins Mental Health Center in Watts around midnight the day of her court appointment on January 8, 2003. "That bitch," Tina said about Wilma. "I'm a whoop that bitch ass! I pay that bitch every time I go to court!" Tina had been unable to get the paperwork she needed to get herself out of her court appointment. So she had feigned symptoms of a breakdown, secured the paperwork, which was duly delivered to her lawyer, missed court, and was released around 1:00 pm that same day. She hadn't cooled down about Wilma, and told Redd, "I'ma go by that bitch house, let that bitch know that, when I go back to court, she ain't there, I'm gonna beat her motherfuckin' ass!"

In a few days, Tina settled down. Of course she couldn't harm Wilma: the woman was too valuable to scare off. When they next spoke, she and Wilma calmly discussed the letters, the dates, and the next court appearance. They talked about Wilma's emotions and Tina's "problem." "I know you deal with a lot of women," Tina said, and admitted that sometimes she just didn't try. She was caught between Black and K-Rok, she said, and had conflicting loyalties.

Tina had always been conflicted about her sexuality. She had never been molested or traumatized in anyway, unless you counted her time as a prostitute. She described her years as K-Rok's hooker as "demoralizing." K-Rok had pimped her out, but he also grew close to her and helped her to learn the game. In the process, Tina had also learned the relationship between California's courts and mental health system. She received court waivers because of her mental instability, and repeated postponement of court dates led her to believe she could avoid a trial altogether.

The requisite theatrics were easy to plan, and Tina related them to Junior. She detailed how she would arrive at court shaking and looking jacked up. She would mess up her hair or put a stocking cap over her head. "It won't be pretty," she said to Junior. Tina didn't confine her bragging about these arrangements to Junior; she told her brother, Clifford, Redd, and Big T. She mentioned her skill at avoiding trial to Tawana. In the process of telling these people, Tina also inadvertently told Special Agent King.

The task force had stumbled across wiretapped phone calls from January 7 between Junior and Tina. Tina was awaiting instructions from someone named Wilma regarding the next day's court appointment and indicated that she was thinking of having someone take her to Augustus Hawkins. Later the same day, King overheard Tina say to Tawana that "the bitch was trippin" and couldn't go to court, and lay out her own plans for checking herself into the hospital that night.

In the meantime, Officer Brooks had arrested Tawana on some charge and taken her to jail. A January 8 phone call featured Tina and Junior talking about Tawana going to jail, and more about "that bitch not going to court." Apparently, Tina had hurt Wilma's feelings by shirking meetings between the two. Tina had told Wilma, "This a business, bitch."

On January 10, 2003, Wilma asked Tina to take a look at the letter she'd typed up for her. She said she loved Tina unconditionally and cared about Tina's life. They discussed the $200 for Tina's fictitious bed rental, which Wilma would "put into the houses." They arranged to fake a date on the letter. The FBI would eventually record eleven phone calls related to Wilma Jones and Tina Fly's manipulation of the state courts by faking mental illness. In 2005, Assistant U.S. Attorney Jennifer Corbet submitted wiretap excerpts of these conversations as part of a rejoinder to Federal Public Defender Phil Deitch's argument that Tina's mental health history should mitigate her sentence for conspiracy drug distribution charges.

By the time of Tina's sentencing in 2005, many Fly Trap targets had been sitting in Los Angeles Metropolitan Detention Center (MDC) for two years, awaiting the outcome of their cases. The majority of the sixteen federal defendants had already taken pleas and were serving time in various federal facilities, most of which were in California. But Tina, Junior, and Juan Lococo faced life. They were the highest-level players and were being tried together. They risked most, came closest to having a full-blown jury trial, and had had the longest stay at MDC.

Originally the list of defendants in *United States v. Edwards* included John Edwards, Juan Lococo, Charlotte Jackson, Tawana Edwards, Brian Favors, Dante Washington, Thomas Adams, Erick Kennedy, and Lincoln Widmore. They were the members of just one of several conspiracies in the case whose participants were to be tried in the federal chambers of the Honorable Gary Klausner. Although Judge Klausner was new to the U.S. District Court's Central Division, he had been sitting on the bench for almost thirty years. He heard Fly Trap's case within a common federal framework: the conspiracy.

Conspiracy qualifies most drug cases for trial in federal court. Two or more individuals who work toward the commission of a crime fall under its purview. Conspiracy trials date back to fourteenth-century England, where they protected innocent people from false accusations by the court. Today, conspiracy charges do the opposite. They are filled with "traps for the unwary and opportunities for the repressor."[1] While charging and proving conspiracies are easy, defending and disproving them present a special problem.

Conspiracy, termed "the prosecutor's darling," is a frequently charged federal crime with enough flexibility to apply to a great variety of behaviors. "It is clear that a conspiracy charge gives the prosecution certain unique advantages and that one who must defend against such a charge bears a particularly heavy burden."[2] Individuals may be prosecuted based on intention rather than outcome—on thoughts or plans rather than actions. In conspiracy cases, the crime is the agreement, not the action. Conspirators need not know one another, nor even be aware of their fellow defendants' identities. Yet the defendants are responsible for one another's behavior. The details of when a person joined a conspiracy do not matter; he or she is still complicit in all of it. Furthermore, a prosecutor only needs to prove tacit agreement between conspiratorial parties rather than a formal one. Whether a crime was actually committed is similarly a minor consideration; only intention is required for prosecution and punishment under conspiracy laws. Rules of evidence are "relaxed" in conspiracy cases to justify the purported secrecy that surrounds conspiratorial acts.[3]

Despite the dangers of criminal conspiracy as a legal mechanism, today's security-focused domestic climate has provided ample opportunity to grow the frequency and ease of conspiracy charges. Conspiracy has been an ideal companion to the drug war, and the lax standards of evidence that federal drug prosecution requires have partly resulted from the historical trajectories of conspiracy laws. Clarence Darrow warned in 1894 that conspiracy has "been the favorite weapon of every tyrant. It is an effort to punish the crime of thought. If there are still any citizens interested in protecting human liberty, let them study the conspiracy laws of the United States."[4]

The powerful but little-known characteristics of conspiracy placed questions in the defendants' minds: How was this possible? Was the government trying to pull something? How could Juan Lococo have known that John Edwards would have turned powder cocaine into crack? How could Kevin Allen be held accountable for other people's behavior if he didn't even know they were involved? Why had some targets received full "conspirator" status when they hadn't been around for most of the alleged conspiracies? How could the government charge Tina for drug deals that she had arranged over the phone but that had never taken place?

The loose definition of conspiracy makes sense of certain of the federal system's more perplexing aspects. "Ghost dope," for example, is an insider (criminal) label for dope that dealers may discuss and plan to sell, but its main distinguishing feature is that it does not exist in the material world.

Ghost dope can become the exclusive basis for the quantity calculations that trigger federal mandatory minimums.

Tina, for example, argues that her sentence was calculated incorrectly thanks to ghost dope. The court counted discussed transactions that had never happened on the street and confused quantities of marijuana with quantities of cocaine or crack—very different substances from the sentencing point of view. The wiretapped phone conversations were the real problem, she says.

> Like, they'll call, somebody calls, "Well, I needs this." Like, instead of they're saying, "well I need a half or a four," they would make it to an amount that's way triple more. And then sometimes we don't even make the arrangement. Like somebody call and, "Well, Tina, I need this or that." And I'm like, "All right, whatever." You know, and I probably don't never take it to them, or they probably never get it. So they used all that against me. Just my phone conversation. And then it wasn't just only that: we used to sell weed, too. So somebody would say, "Well, I want a half ounce." They think they're talking about coke and they'll put that, and it be weed, you understand. See by reading all of the discovery, *I* knew. I knew, you know.

Tina had painstakingly read the discovery and knew where the problems were. As she stewed in the MDC, her depression returned, and prescription pharmaceuticals took the place of the illegal drugs with which she would have normally self-medicated.[5]

Tina had been on drugs before her criminal drug history began at age fourteen. She could not recall what doctors had prescribed her at nine, nor did she remember any of the behavior-modification drugs they had given her as a pre- and early teen. Her mother says Tina took Ritalin to counter her hyperactivity. Later, it was risperidone, an antipsychotic; valproic acid, a mood stabilizer also used for epileptic and schizophrenic patients; and Prozac for depression. Young Tina went to therapy and attended special schools. Tina eventually joined mainstream school but dropped out in eleventh grade after becoming pregnant with Tawana. She had felt conflicted about the baby, but Junior had refused to let her have an abortion.

When Tina turned eighteen, the now mother of two began to use PCP. This new drug mimicked a manic state and made her feel powerful and happy in the face of Junior's more controlling tendencies. Two years later, in 1984, she began to use powder and crack cocaine. For the next twenty years, crack became the center of her world. All the AFDC money she received for her two kids went to support her habit. The girls went to stay with their maternal and paternal grandmothers. Tina had by then become a prostitute, entered and left hourly rate motels, and made no effort to keep her mind intact except to survive. Her family and friends began to wonder how much of Tina's "mentalness," as her mom calls it, had to do with Tina, and how much with the drugs.

Tina's mental health history shows an all-too-common intersection between legal and illegal drug use, mental illness, and prison time. According to a 2006 Bureau of Justice Statistics report, over half of all prison and jail inmates have mental health problems. Approximately 75 percent of women in local jails qualify as mentally ill, as do 73 percent in state prisons and 61 percent in federal lockups. Statistics for men average around 50 percent. Bureau of Justice Statistics researchers found that a community-based mental health facility would be a more effective (and less costly) place for these individuals to go than prison.[6]

A flawed attempt to deinstitutionalize the mental health industry has led to these high numbers of incarcerated mentally ill people. This move temporally and thematically coincided with economic deindustrialization in U.S. inner cities. Deinstitutionalization began in the 1960s, gained momentum in the 1980s, and was fairly complete by the 1990s.[7] Few were sad to see the old mental institutions go. These often barbaric facilities had high rates of abuse by staff, widespread overmedication, and a penchant for treatments such as electroshock therapy. But the community treatment centers slated to replace the old hospitals never materialized. A lack of funding and the stigma attached to mental illness, combined with economic restructuring and an ongoing housing crisis, placed unprecedented numbers of mentally ill people on the streets, and in our jails and prisons. Jails became the new mental health facilities. Today, the Los Angeles County Jail and New York's Riker's Island compete as the largest mental health providers in the country.

Inmates with mental health issues are more likely to have concurrent substance abuse problems, participate in the illegal economy, perpetrate violence, have trouble following institutional rules, and serve longer sentences than non–mentally ill people.[8]

During her stay at the MDC, Tina suffered from severe depression. Her body became covered with hives. Public Defender Deitch argued in Tina's sentencing memorandum that her previous and ongoing mental health status should constitute a mitigating factor in her sentencing. The memo was exhaustive and well researched. It cited relevant precedent and ex-

hibits demonstrating repeated diagnoses such as "borderline mentally re-
tarded," "illiterate," "simplistic," "depressive disorder," "schizophrenia,"
"chronic paranoid," and "organic brain syndrome secondary to substance
abuse." These diagnoses lent credibility to Deitch's arguments regarding
Tina's impaired judgment, her inability to live independently or make independent decisions, and the ease with which others in the conspiracy,
such as Allen and Edwards, controlled her.

The U.S. attorneys would have none of it. Assistant U.S. Attorney Corbet knew firsthand how someone's background could shift the focus of a
case away from the crime and onto a defendant's personal history. Corbet had worked as the Central Division's coordinator for crimes against
children and had seen the worst criminals attempt to excuse their horrific
actions with such tactics. The voices of crime victims in drug cases were
largely absent—and they could be trumped by a defendant's stories of
abuse or neglect. One has to draw the line somewhere, and Corbet would
not let Tina's mental health status become a get-out-of-jail-free card. Furthermore, she and her fellow assistant U.S. attorney Kevin Rosenberg had
their own trump card: Wilma Jones.

> July 1, 2002
>
> I Wilma Jones Program Administrator where Charlotte Jackson is living
> am writing this letter to inform the courts that Charlotte Jackson is unable to
> appear in court due to a emotional breakdown and she is heavily sedated. I
> Wilma Jones as the Program Administrator will make sure that she be in court
> on her next appearance. The Doctor will see her at Kedren Community Mental
> Health Center again in three (3) weeks July 25, 2002. Please feel free to contact
> me for further information.

*   *   *

Nothing in Deitch's memorandum detailing Tina's illnesses could compete with the prosecution's succinct recitation of the Jones–Fly connection. Corbet and Rosenberg argued that Tina's time in jail, her time in
treatment, or her court dates had not deterred her from running a drug
distribution enterprise. Deitch had little room left to counter that mentally ill people are chronically involved in the illegal economy as a result of their illness, that some evidence shows children on Ritalin to be
more susceptible to stimulant abuse later in life, or that Tina's mental illness may have bolstered her delusion that she could successfully manipulate the court system. The U.S. attorneys were firm and convincing: Tina

needed to be held accountable for her actions to the maximum the government would allow.

The U.S. attorneys' arguments anticipated a new wave of concern in the legal community. Following *Blakely* and *Booker*, two key U.S. Supreme Court decisions, judges could now hand down sentences below the government's formerly inviolate guidelines. The courts adopted the guidelines to eliminate unintentional bias in sentencing, but as time passed, it was clear that the guidelines also worked "to eliminate judicial leniency."[9] Judges' hands were essentially tied until *Booker* and *Blakely*, and many were forced to deliver predetermined sentences that they believed, in some cases, to be inappropriate. After *Booker* and *Blakely*, the guidelines became advisory rather than regulatory, and attorneys' arguments took on greater importance.[10]

The federal sentencing guidelines are depicted on a step-and-stairs chart featuring zones A through D, with offense levels of 1 through 43, and criminal history categories of I through VI. Numbers designating ranges of months begin with a modest 0–6 and end with life sentences. Life starts at zone D, level 38, criminal history category V. Convicted individuals call longer sentences "jersey numbers," or "defense football numbers," which K-Rok explains are popular references to the double-digit years commonly doled out for drug crimes.

> That's the most significant thing, especially for people involved with no violence. You have to do *some* time. But they giving them defense football numbers—they giving you jersey numbers. That's crazy. And nobody was hurt. Then they get people doing crimes against children and they get way less time. That's a gross disproportion. They giving bank robbers less time. You got more of a chance to hurt somebody robbing that bank than me standing on that corner. I don't know how or when they figured out how that makes sense.

The crack cocaine panic that had occurred during the Reagan era was part media scare, part epidemiological fantasy. People believed that crack cocaine was the most violent drug yet discovered and that it produced more pathology, was more addictive, and had created a generation of crack babies who would produce even more problems for society. Nothing about the resulting 100:1 sentencing disparity is nuanced. Far from the only travesty, 100:1 is the preeminent symbol of a failed drug war whose skewed sentencing practices have carved out public life and racial politics in the United States for nearly twenty-five years.

Before 2010's Fair Sentencing Act, the U.S. Sentencing Commission made many formal recommendations to end the discrepancies in the sentencing of those convicted of crimes involving powder versus crack cocaine. "Whatever anecdotes and stereotypes caused Congress to treat crack cases so harshly in 1986 are no longer valid, if they ever were. Violent crack dealers should be punished for their violence; non-violent crack dealers should not be punished on the false assumption that all crack dealers are violent."[11] As a drug of the poor, crack tends to be sold in more violent street markets to and by people of color. Powder is sold behind the scenes to (at the time of the initial war on drugs) mostly wealthier whites. Sentencing Commission statistics demonstrate that by 2000, roughly 85 percent of crack prosecutions have been of African Americans (with 9 percent Latino and 5.6 percent white), although in fact crack users were 64 percent white, and just 26 percent were African American.[12]

Until the Fair Sentencing Act of 2010, constitutional changes to the 100:1 disparity largely fell on proving intent to discriminate. International law supported by several U.S. Supreme Court justices ultimately provided some impetus for change because it "requires the elimination of discrimination not only when there is discriminatory intent, but also where there is unjustified discriminatory effect."[13]

For most of the Fly Trap defendants, the federal system came as a shock. They were undereducated about federal law and sentencing disparities, and in general about the nature of federal interest in their neighborhoods. The FBI's decision to target two "average" gang neighborhoods surprised the defendants. They beat themselves up for not knowing better and for believing they understood the risks they took. They did not know—and could hardly believe after their hearings—the lengthy sentences associated with drug conspiracy laws.

Conspiracy laws stem from the belief that groups of people have the capacity to do more harm than individuals, and that an individual is less likely to change his or her mind and back out of a crime if beholden to others. Conspiracy law retains the power to render equivalent people, crime, intent, planning, and fruition. Advances in technology enhance this power.

Law enforcement officials who specialize in conspiracy cases concentrate their efforts on segments of society they believe likely to produce prosecutable conspiracies. Conspiracy can thus be seen as a "status crime," since a person's social status may determine whether law enforcement prosecutes them.[14] The importance of social status in defining existing power relationships renders this process far from neutral.

Aside from the potential for abuse when used against minority and other groups, a true conspiracy, according to Ninth Circuit Court judge Gould, can persist through its prosecution: "Conspiracies pose other special dangers. Unlike individual criminal action, which comes to an end upon the capture of the criminal, collective criminal action has a life of its own. Like the Hydra of Greek mythology, the conspiracy may survive the destruction of its parts unless the conspiracy is completely destroyed. For even if some or many conspirators are imprisoned, others may remain at large, free to recruit others eager to break the law and to pursue the conspiracy's illegal ends."[15] The charges leveled against the Fly Trap defendants simultaneously rewarded and punished their acceptance of responsibility. In penalizing collective accountability, conspiracy charges run opposite of boot-strap ideology, in which persons must accept responsibility for the conduct of others, for crimes that never happened, or for drugs that do not exist.

Families in the thick of courtroom drama enter a system of drug-related sentencing that seems entirely foreign. Those who work within the federal system and are familiar with its daily jargon and strange calculations may cease to notice just how little sense their judgments make from the outside. The people I interviewed clearly expected the courts to prioritize criminal acts in the same way that they did personally. They believed that their own rankings of a crime's severity on the street ought to translate into the length of a person's sentence.

They also pointed out, as do legal scholars and activists, that white-collar criminals cost society far more and get much less time.[16] Even in light of common racial biases, the defendants and their families still found the sentencing aspects of the case baffling. Ghetto families and neighborhoods have adapted to deal with certain amounts of prison time: the three-to-five-year sentence, perhaps eighteen to twenty-four months, maybe even six or eight years. But the federal mandatory minimums break a system of fictive and blood kinship already made flexible by the pervasive problem of prison time in ghetto communities. The minimums force people to rewrite affiliations that have been developed in part to deal with ties between state prison and the street.

Most if not all of the families and clients had difficulty communicating with their lawyers, and they did not understand how and which decisions influenced length of sentence. They did not understand the burden of proof, nor that after they pled guilty, the government no longer had to prove anything beyond a reasonable doubt.

Juan Lococo, who received jersey number 22, had desperately attempted to represent himself in the final days of his case. He had felt the case slipping away and figured he could do no worse than his lawyer. His sister described the humiliation she felt at the hands of the court. "They laughed at my brother like he was a dog," she says.

> And then the people in court, like the police officers and stuff, they would laugh at us in our face. Because my brother, he lost it for a moment. 'Cause they made, they forced him to sign it. "Either you sign it or you're going to jury and you're gonna be found guilty and you're gonna be in here for life." That's what they basically told him. My brother, he, he went, kind of psycho. They had to tie him down and put handcuffs all over him. I told him he had to calm down. And they took him back, you know. He was crying like a little boy. And they were laughing at him. They were laughing at him. And it's like, it's sad because it's your own race laughing at you. Because one of the officers that got him, he was Mexican. He was Mexican and he was one of the ones really laughing at him. They were *laughing* at him. You know and it's just very, very bad.

King remembered the laughter too. Lococo had claimed ineffective council while representing himself, and everyone had to chuckle about the fact that he was declaring himself to be ineffective. King also remembered something else, though, which he mentioned to me as a final, open exchange between two parties. At one point during the proceedings, Lococo called King over to ask his advice: "What do you think I should do?" With the mutual respect implied in that question, King felt square. He could still wake up and look himself in the mirror, as his dad had said all those years ago.

Lococo's own memory of this conversation is a blur, one among many intensely stressful moments during Fly Trap's culmination. What he did remember made him feel the opposite of square. His overall experience in the federal courts led directly to his belief that the government was lying. To Lococo, the case was not illegal per se but, in his words, unlawful. He especially took issue with the quantity calculations and the fact that the federal courts require no hard evidence in order to calculate a sentence.

> We are guilty, we all sold cocaine, and Tina and John did sell crack. But not in the amounts they said we did. Is it right that in order to maximize the sentence of certain individuals guilty of breaking the law, the government breaks just as many to not only convict but maximize their sentence?

John Edwards was equally suspicious of what was happening.

Do you know there's a difference between *rock* cocaine and *powder* cocaine? . . . 50 grams of rock cocaine get you 10 years (black men and women) 100 kilos of powder cocaine get you maybe 5–10 years (white men and women). Now look at the difference. I'm not crying out to you, but where is justice at? We deserve some punishment, but not like this. Because this system is destroy our family and they really are. Don't just throw people lives away. By throwing our lives away, [you don't] help the situation or the problem. I hate to give up on my case but my lawyer is not a lawyer. A lawyer finds ways to break a case open but my lawyer didn't do anything. God knows, I went to the law library busted my tail off. And I know in my *heart* that the government broke the law just like I did and two wrongs doesn't make a right.

Lococo was also outraged by Tina Fly and CS-1's close relationship: that Crystal had exchanged drugs for sex with most of the targets, had been Tina's lover, and had even lived with Tina. Had such facts been in evidence, Lococo asserted, the whole case would have been compromised. Lococo also blames Officer Brooks for his testimony that the defendants' race made them predisposed to turn cocaine, which carries the much lighter sentence, into crack, which carries the much heavier sentence.

John, Tina, and myself were sentenced for distributing over 1½ kilos of cocaine base (crack), *but* the government never seized over 1½ kilos of cocaine base. We were sentenced for crimes we should've *been thinking* about doing, since we did have powder cocaine. To quote Officer Brooks (LAPD) who got on the stand at my sentencing hearing, I should be sentenced to distributing over 1½ kilos of crack, because since I sold powder cocaine to Tina Jackson and since Tina was, I quote, "a black gang member from South Central," I should have known what she would do with powder cocaine. So not only should I have thought about turning powder cocaine into crack but because Tina was black and from South Central I should've also known what her mind was thinking. Check the transcripts yourself, I couldn't believe that in a U.S. federal courtroom, a black police officer said this and *no one*, not even the judge, objected to it.

Such a scene may seem inherently objectionable, but recalculating quantities of powder into quantities of crack in order to maximize the sentence is a widely used tactic with plenty of legal precedent.[17] According to the U.S. attorneys, "the distribution of crack cocaine clearly establishes their knowledge that the powder cocaine involved in their offenses would be converted to crack cocaine. As a result, the court should convert the amounts of powder cocaine involved in the defendants' conspiracy into crack cocaine for sentencing purposes."[18]

This line of thinking hinged in part on a "cookie" that Juan Lococo had manufactured to demonstrate a rocked-up sample of his powder. As was the usual arrangement, Lococo had provided it to Jackson, who had then given it to Edwards. Police confiscated the cookie from Edwards's apartment on October 30, 2002. All three defendants were eventually charged with possession of the 993 grams of powder cocaine seized at Edwards's residence the day of Operation Fly Trap. They were also all charged with the cookie. In some measure, the cookie proved their collective knowledge that others would turn the powder they sold into crack cocaine on the streets.

In a courtroom, formally converting quantities of powder cocaine into crack cocaine for sentencing requires its own special formula. In the real world, crack is approximately 10 percent baking soda. With this 10 percent in mind, the courts found that, to be fair, one kilogram of cocaine must be recalculated as only 900 grams of crack. Before 2010, a kilogram of powder cocaine would normally place a defendant at base level 26, which carries a sentencing range of 63–150 months, or 5.25–12.5 years, depending on the circumstances.[19] When recalculated, however, the kilogram of powder—despite equaling a lesser quantity of drugs—now places the same defendant at base level 36. This ten-level addition now makes the sentencing range a whopping 188–405 months, or 15.6–33.75 years—between two and three times as much time as the sentence associated with powder cocaine.

Consequently, Lococo, Edwards, and Jackson were all charged with possession of 2,953.51 grams of powder cocaine, but after the conversion this amount became 2.66 kilograms of crack. The initial quantity would have earned them 6.5–14.5 years, but that amount of crack carries a possible life sentence. The defendants went from level 28, which begins at 78 months, to level 38, which begins at 235 months and ends at life. The U.S. attorneys indicated that "the government believes that significant sentences are appropriate and necessary in order to adequately protect the public from these defendants, deter the defendants and other members of the public from engaging in similar crimes, avoid unnecessary sentencing disparities among all the defendants in these cases, and promote respect for the law."[20]

Basing sentencing on a drug not even in evidence severely compromises justice. That the courts do so by enhancing legislation regarded as openly racist is unconscionable. This practice does precisely the opposite of what the U.S. attorneys claim. Without quantity recalculation, Tina, John, and Junior would have served sentences similar to those of the other defendants instead of their 25, 22, and 27 years, respectively. The law is to blame for this disparity in sentencing, since it overinflates the sentencing value of crack over powder. The defendants' collective removal to prison for more than a decade would have served any commonsense, public safety need. As for deterrence, recalculating quantities of powder into crack is such a convoluted practice that a working knowledge of the law becomes impossible. A warped sense of justice calculated 10 percent less of a drug was worth at that time 100 percent more in sentencing. Far from promoting respect for the law, this kind of practice undermines that respect at every turn.

Conspiracy drug laws now represent a case in which policy no longer matches the popular understanding—even among society's most disenfranchised—of what is or should be going on in the courts. The more the defendants learned about their sentences, the more they became convinced that the actions of the federal system could not possibly be legitimate. They knew the government *had* to be lying. Most felt they had been the victims of government wrongdoing, corner cutting, or data falsification. But I found only two instances in which claims of corner cutting and falsification held water. The other complaints stemmed from misunderstanding of the federal courts, the nature of conspiracy, the burden of proof, and the legal but unjust things the government can do to build evidence, secure convictions, and maximize sentences.

Those sentenced to federal mandatory minimums have long had one way out: giving information. Whereas contextual factors such as use of a minor, prior convictions, or a leadership role can lessen or add to a sentence by specific amounts of time, snitching has no such limitation. It can shave a few years off a sentence or do away with a prosecution entirely. Tina was in it too deep for such a thing, she says. "Who would I tell on? Myself?"

To Tina's base level 38, the U.S. attorneys wanted to add 4 for her role as a leader, 2 for her use of a minor, and then subtract 2 for her acceptance of responsibility. With a potential level of 42, Tina faced a life sentence. She eventually took a plea for twenty-five years at level 36. Tina had refused to give information—true for several of the Fly Trap defendants.

Tawana decided to "tell on herself" and discuss her role in what the court already knew about her family. She refused to give any more information. She begged the court to give her her parents' sentences and let them go. She tried to keep her parents' names out of anything else she told the authorities.

> I'm ready to accept my responsibility, 'cause I know why I'm here. I don't know what anybody else did, but I know why *I'm* here. *I* know what *I* did. And that was it. But what they got to saying was, "You need to tell on your mom and your daddy, you need to tell us this, you need to tell us that." And I'm like, "Tell y'all *what* about my momma and my daddy? That's stuff that you already know. Only thing I could tell you is I did what I had to do. But I can't tell you nothing about Jackson or about Edwards. I can tell you what I did, but I can't tell you about what they did." And then my attorney, he like pressuring me a little bit, he's like, "Tell on your dad then." "If I tell on my dad," I say, "How is that gonna benefit me? What am I gonna get out of it if I tell on my dad?" I say, "You know what? Matter of fact, just give me whatever time y'all are gonna give me and just send me on by my way." And I just asked 'em, I kept saying, "Why don't you send my mom and my dad home, and let me do they time?" 'Cause I ain't got nothing to lose. I say, "I really, I don't got no kids, I don't have nothing. So just send them home." And they was like, "No, you going to jail too. You just like your mom and your dad." [pause] And I *never* been to jail before. *Never.* I just. This my first time, being in prison. And it's like . . . it's like . . . sad to be here. And there ain't no telling when my mom or my dad gonna come home or nothing.

When I first met her in person at FCI Dublin, Tawana was twenty-six, soft-spoken, and angry. Although her record was clean on the outside, the moment she entered prison she started fighting other women. She had shoved another inmate through a glass window at MDC, and the months before her mother arrived at FCI Dublin were filled with violent incidents for which she got more time. She just wanted to fight, she said. Tina's arrival at Dublin calmed Tawana down, and from then on her record was clean. By the time I met Tawana, she was due to get out the next year with 85 percent time served.

> I lost my family behind this stuff. I don't have anything or anyone to help me through this. I got 7 years, 3 months. I don't have a dime, no money. . . . They gave me too much time. It's hard for me, my first time I been in trouble and this

is what I get. This is hard times for me, and it hurt when both of your parents
are in jail with you.

In addition to the loss of her parents, Tawana's entire community had been
ripped apart by snitching. Her mother's associates and her own homeboys
had betrayed her and had violated the code they all valued. Tawana worried about what would happen when she saw the people who had given
information out on the streets after her release. She said she wasn't going
to trust anybody.

'Cause those are the people that I grew up with, from babies to now. And you
knew the consequences of selling drugs. You know if you get busted, don't say
nothing. But no, you gonna say something about me and my mom and my dad.
I don't want to go back to that same environment because I know me. You
know, because I be like, if I see someone or something like "you snitched on
my momma." But I'm going to leave it alone. I'm angry, but I'm not going to let
her [Tina] or my dad see it, you know. But I'm angry. Very angry.

Tawana had been charged with possession and sale of forty-five grams of
crack cocaine, which included the controlled buy of powder with Crystal
and five grams of crack they said they found in her apartment. (Tawana contested the veracity of these five grams.) The guidelines proposed twenty-
five years, but Tawana took a deal for ten. They took away three points for
accepting responsibility. Although he could have given her less, the judge
opted to give her 108 months. He said she knew more than she let on.
Tawana believed that, when she was released from jail, "they going to be
following me. I honestly think they not going to leave me alone."

K-Rok had never thought he would snitch. He equated snitches with
homosexuals, whom he loathed. But with life imprisonment over his head,
K-Rok rethought his opinion. His actions, he says, were part of a broader
game being played by nearly everyone in the case. "I did what I did because of the way the whole thing feeds back on itself. Fifteen, sixteen
people told. And they expect me to be the stand-up guy and do the time
for everybody because of who I am in the neighborhood?" Tina regarded
K-Rok's decision to give information a deep betrayal. "I loved Rok," she
said.

They gave Rok a way out. He tell on Big Man and me. But he had been telling.
They ran up and they spy. He was telling before they come and picked us up.

Before they picked us up in June, he had been telling. He had told everything. When they ran up in Black house, and they tooked him to jail. And let him out and didn't have to bail out or nothing. Just let him go. Feds were on us already. And see the feds started with K-Rok. That's how they got on me.

Conspiracies force people to narrate a space between the acceptance and denial of responsibility. Both targets and authorities desire to pinpoint the inception or center of a conspiracy. Tracing back the information that leads to inclusion in a conspiracy can become something near to an obsession for targets—akin to finding the single "leader" of a gang for authorities. Conspiracies often have no clear center, so attempting to follow the thread of how authorities came to information was a way for the Fly Trap defendants and their families to reframe blame and responsibility.

K-Rok had decided to cooperate when he learned he faced a possible life sentence. To him, this was "bullshit" since he had been caught "without one salt-grain of drugs." By turning informant, he only received ten years. He still considers himself dedicated to his hood even though he has technically forsaken it. He also snitched, he says, because the system was unjust to "Africans in America." "Sometimes I feel great about it. Because I saved my life. But sometimes I feel like I should have kept it gangsta. But if I had kept it gangsta, I wouldn't have been able to see my kids again. I know I can't never go back to what I really love. It's like a mandate: I got no choice. I have to make a change in my life. I used to hate snitches. I don't feel that way no more." K-Rok still has some juice in the neighborhood among select individuals. He loves the streets as he loves himself; they are part of him. But the toxic elements in street culture, he well recognizes, may encourage anyone over a certain age to seek out a change. In this case, snitching became the act that forced him to make this change.

Loyalty and betrayal keep necessary company within the context of lengthy federal sentences. The cultural imperatives of gang membership are compromised, yet even these compromises fail to undermine years of gang socialization, the inscriptions of identity on the body, a hatred for law enforcement, and the use of prison to gain prestige. K-Rok was already marginal to gang life, but he was still beholden to gang mores. There is now "paperwork" on K-Rok, Mark Brooks says, which doesn't bode well for him. "Gang members don't take police reports as gospel, but they do take court transcripts as gospel. The presentence reports are gospel to them. Once they get the transcripts that a person testified in open court about another gang member, they will kill him for that." A presentence report is a document used to determine the length of a person's sentence. The report measures the quantity of drugs and type of crime committed versus a person's criminal history and willingness to accept responsibility, and any "help" he or she may have given to authorities. The report determines where a person should fall within the sentencing guidelines.

While awaiting trial, K-Rok was at risk that gang members, through their routine discovery and transcript readings, would determine that he had breached their loyalty. Once in the penitentiary, however, he risked even more. In most prisons, veteran inmates force new arrivals to produce presentence reports within a designated time frame in order to determine whether the new inmate has snitched, or is a rapist or other sex offender. Any departures from the sentencing framework (which is well known), such as a sealed record, which usually indicates cooperation, or an inmate's inability or unwillingness to produce the document, are likely indicators that a person has exchanged information for time. When a determination is made, K-Rok says, an inmate will then be threatened with or become a victim of violence, which forces the inmate off the main line and into protective custody.

> It's a must that you have your paperwork if you want to walk on the main line. You can go through the courts [to get the presentence report]. They can't tell you you can't fight your case. So you allowed to have all that paperwork to continue to fight that case for your freedom. You can have your family send it in or have somebody look up your docket for you and get it; there's a number of ways to do it. If it's sealed, that's another thing that will alert a person that something is wrong. A lot of yards is like that. It's ways around it. But if a person is enforcing it, you have to deal with it. You cannot be on the line without it. It is scary, especially for a person like me.

By forcing new inmates to make public their presentence reports, veteran inmates are able to enforce codes of silence, loyalty, and exclusion both inside and outside of prison. In prison, known snitches generally live in exile, relegated to special units that protectively house them with other vilified criminals, such as homosexuals or sex offenders.

Here the self-perpetuating system of incarceration is used by the people it incarcerates to become a source of social power. A system designed to destroy criminal and gang networks instead reconstitutes them behind bars. Prison walls stop very little: not drugs, not gangs, not violence. Indeed, the drug trade is so enmeshed with prisons that "American society could not be drug-free even if it were completely unfree."[21]

*   *   *

John Edwards had misunderstood the enormity of the sentence that awaited him: he thought his level was 32, his lawyer said it was 36, and the U.S. attorneys were arguing for a level 38. Junior had thought his plea was between ten and twenty years for fifty grams of crack. A level 32 would equal no more than twenty years. His lawyer tried to argue down to level 36 because Junior had grown up in a drug-infested environment. He was a good father to his children and a good fixture in his community. Corbet countered that Junior had chosen to lead a life of crime in a neighborhood where not everyone became a drug dealer. He had involved at least one of his children in his operations. He had profited behind the scenes by spreading dangerous drugs in the community.

Judge Klausner had carefully read Junior's three-page letter to the court and had taken into account multiple contextual factors as well as the sentencing guidelines. Instead of the government's request of a level 38, Judge Klausner decided to give Junior a level 36. He knew Junior was remorseful and that his family depended on him. He even opted to sentence on the lowest end of the 324- to 405-month scale for that level and declared Junior's sentence to be 324 months. Junior's jersey number was 27.

In the face of his twenty-seven years, Junior turned to the one entity he knew he could count on: God. Junior had always prayed with his family, but after his sentencing, Junior rarely expressed himself without reference to the Lord. Junior became known as someone "into Jesus" at FCI Victorville, where he was serving out his term.

I asked Junior whether he thought his twenty-seven years was fair and what had gone through his mind when the sentence had been handed down.

God is good all the time. He is worthy of all praise. He is God alone. He is the living God. He is the Judge of all. Yes, I think it was totally unfair. With the guidelines as advisory only, my plea was from 10 to 20 years, not from 20 to 30, which is still a long time. There wasn't nothing I could do or say. Is the system unfair for punishing me for the crime I committed? Read Romans 13: 1–4. My appeal lawyer is filing my two-point reduction, plus my 2255 [motion to reduce sentence] is being prepared. God gives us the resources that we need, but our trust is in God the Father, Our Lord and Savior Jesus Christ. God has the final word.

The passage Junior referred to reads, "But if thou do that which is evil, be afraid; for he beareth not the sword in vain: for he is the minister of God, a revenger to execute wrath upon him that doeth evil."

I asked Junior whether he considered drug dealing to be truly evil, in as much as evil according to Romans requires one to submit to punishment by God without resistance.

We put ourselves in a position to be judged for our wrongdoings. That's the government's job—to punish evildoers such as myself. There is a point in time when things must come to an end. I thank God this happened, because it could have been a lot worse. The time I received is a bit much. I cry out to our Heavenly Father for His mercy and His mercy only. When I was a drug dealer, I hurt a lot of people. Drugs make people do all types of crimes to support their addiction. I was a big part of that. I regret the things I did to our Heavenly Father's children. We are all God's children. Selling drugs was totally wrong. I was really tired of dealing drugs. God knew I was crying out, but I didn't know who to cry to. God saved me from being separated from Him. Thank you Jesus Christ our Lord.

By this time, Junior was engaged in a conflict between his personal status and his legal status. Legally, he was still in appeals, but personally he had already squared himself with his Lord and savior. He had accepted his punishment as a means to bring him closer to God and to prevent him from further harming God's children. Despite having embraced his status as a wrongdoer in God's eyes, he remained in a painful legal limbo, which prevented him from fully accepting the propriety of his sentence. This was particularly true when the 100:1 crack versus cocaine disparity was rectified to 18:1. Junior knew the laws under which he had been sentenced were unjust, and now potential retroactivity could impact him along with thousands of others convicted in the old way.

Junior's family members paid serious attention to his newfound spiritual strength. As with many penitent prisoners, Junior wanted to forsake all things material—money, sex, drugs, gangs. His most sincere desire was to achieve right in this world. "When I was going to see him at the MDC," Renee says, "we would actually—well, he would actually sit there and give me Bible study."

And then all that I go through on the streets, when I go see him, he would make me feel better about myself. He kept a smile on his face when he was the one in there going through it—going through the motions after what had happened to them and my mom. He was keeping me strong. . . . Then I be doing the same with him, "Do you know that, brother, I remember you before you went in, you know you had a little bit of this church up under you, but you weren't so deep with it like you are now." [pause] "Well what do these twenty—do this twenty-seven years register to you? Or is that why you talk about God so much cause you don't want to see these twenty-seven years that they gave you? I want to know how you actually feel. Cause me, I can't sit. Twenty-seven years—I want to know. Are we gonna still be alive? How many people gonna leave this earth before you come home?"

Renee's inability to have a serious conversation with Junior without mention of his extreme faith furthered her anguish. For Junior and his family, God had always represented an everyday source of strength, but now it represented division as well. "Everybody has their God to serve, you know," says a family friend. "But that kind of stuff can turn you into a really insane person. Because you can't even talk. You can't express yourself without bringing God into the conversation. That can be too much. That's not a good sign. People of that sort sometimes end up losing their mind."

While arrests and courtrooms can still be considered family affairs, prison represents a dissolution of hope and regular family life. For Junior and other prisoners like him, religion counters the ongoing "attack against the self" embedded in the experience of incarceration.[22]

A little insanity, it turns out, is a pretty sane response to the conditions of incarceration. Studies have repeatedly shown how the structure of prison punishment foments not only violence but mental instability as well. The United States' use of solitary confinement alone has been grounds for condemnation by global human rights organizations.

Whether he had lost his mind or had simply retreated to a place he could trust, the one thing Junior did lose was his appeal. The Ninth Circuit affirmed his sentence, and, in a decision we jokingly referred to as the *Supreme Court v. the Supreme Being*, America's highest court denied his petition for review. His case would eventually be kicked back to Judge Klausner. Junior, among other things, simply did not understand his original plea. The day of his original sentencing hearing on July 13, 2005:

EDWARDS: Wasn't my deal from ten to twenty years?

KLAUSNER: No. The plea agreement that was entered into and was explained at the time of the taking of the plea, it's a mandatory minimum of at least twenty years and could be up to life in prison.

EDWARDS: Sir, I was misunderstood. You said from ten to twenty years, no more than twenty years.

KLAUSNER: If you feel you misunderstand you can make the proper motions for reconsideration.

EDWARDS: Excuse me. Fifty grams of crack cocaine, that's level 32, right?

KLAUSNER: The amount . . .

EDWARDS: My charge was fifty grams of crack cocaine, sir.

KLAUSNER: I know what your charge was. I know what the facts before the court are. I know what the facts were you admitted to at the time of sentencing. All of that was taken into consideration and the court gave the appropriate sentence under the guidelines under 3553 of the United States Code. If you feel you were misled or there's some problem . . .

EDWARDS: I have been misled.

KLAUSNER: You can make those motions. Also, you have to exercise that right within ten days.

EDWARDS: Sir, ten days?

KLAUSNER: Appellate rights. If you want to file an appeal you have to do it within ten days.

EDWARDS: Sir, I was very misled.

KLAUSNER: Make those motions. I would be happy to hear them.

EDWARDS: My level should be level 32 for the fifty grams of crack cocaine.

KLAUSNER: If you feel that it's an improper sentence or if you feel that . . .

EDWARDS: Can I explain?

KLAUSNER: . . .you've been misled you can file a written motion.

EDWARDS: Sir, listen to me. Sir, they dropped all my counts. Sir, listen.

KLAUSNER: The court will be in recess.

Fruit of the Poison Tree

Simple concrete barricades surround the U.S. Courthouse on Spring Street. Upon entering, one presents identification and slides a purse or briefcase through the x-ray machine. Deep green terrazzo floors and orange marble-lined walls in the lobby form the backdrop for two statues carved in pale gray stone. *Young Lincoln* is shirtless, with a broad face. He hooks an outsized thumb casually through the waistband of his pants. Directly across from him is *Law*, a woman with similarly large features. Her left hand rests on a tablet containing a quotation from Abraham Lincoln: "No law is stronger than is the public sentiment where it is to be enforced."[1] As one moves into the depths of the building, terrazzo soon becomes flecked linoleum; the chandeliers overhead are quickly reduced to fluorescent tubes.

Down the street, in front of the Roybal Federal Building on Judge John Aiso Street, stands another statue.[2] Four silhouettes with bodies full of holes are cut of silver metal, measuring several stories high. Children like to dart around them, poking fists and arms through the holes, weaving in and out of legs. Inside, the judges' names are emblazoned on their chambers in permanent lettering. Here is no run-down, rickety-elevatored county facility, no daily grind of dingy off-white and flickering lights. Here is a place where justice is rich. No wonder defendants call it the "Royal Ball" building. Although the public can watch, participation here is by invitation only.

The United States Department of Justice employs over 1,400 lawyers across the country. This vast legal machine churns through federal crimes that can act as a great equalizer. Few middle-class white families frequent the visiting rooms of state-run lockups. But just as the DOJ upsets state hierarchies of punishment by striking at white-collar crime, embezzlement, and Ponzi schemes, its commitment to the war on drugs produces a more common hierarchy of race, class, and the law.

I have written this book to tell a story about the entrance of gangs into the federal sentencing arena. I wanted to represent opposing viewpoints and to provide contexts for understanding how those viewpoints make sense. The Fly Trap stories touch on many issues in criminal justice, pointing out flaws in the system from surveillance to sentencing. Nearly all of those flaws inadvertently erode informal networks of control, reciprocity, and mutual support. But this book stops at a certain point. The targets' experiences of incarceration are beyond this treatment. Tina and Tawana, for example, each received $800 as part of a $25 million settlement in San Bernardino County, just east of Los Angeles, in a lawsuit involving invasive group strip-searches. Missing also are the challenges of prisoner reentry. Tawana was released from prison in 2008 with the economy in crisis, and finding a job, with little support, was a condition of her supervised release. As of this writing, she is living with her aunt and has sporadic employment as an in-home care worker. Other targets wound up back on the streets and back in the game.

Mark Brooks says he now knows how to dismantle a gang. Fly Trap for him was a learning tool. He sees its limitations. He sees how and where they could have done better. They knew some things, yes, but there was so much more to uncover. His primary lessons included two things. First, he learned that by forcing gang members to violate their own codes through snitching, you could embarrass a gang in front of its peers. This embarrassment is key, he said, because no other gangs will want to deal with them after that. Second, he said, you have to go after the locations. Find out where they hang out, where they conduct their business, attack those locations, and leave them with nowhere else to go.

> I understand a lot more now. I know what's going on down there. I understand the people a lot more. It's a serious cancer down there. The cancer is a way of thinking. The community accepts a lot of bad things. YGs [young gangsters] commit murder, and they come back to the neighborhood like heroes. The gang and what they stand for is the cancer: it's not doing anything but promote gang violence. For the project people to accept something like that is a cancer. You jump in thirteen, fourteen year olds and put a gun in their hands. That's the cancer—that they accepting what's going on down there, and nobody's saying, this ain't right.

After the Fly Trap takedown, Brooks and King were involved in another federal task force in the 6-9 East Coast Crips neighborhood that put this lesson into practice. After the takedown, authorities decided to evict every resident—black or Latino, gang or nongang, young or old—from the apartment building in which the 6-9s had had a stranglehold. After a three-year period, Brooks claims, no one can find the gang. A later federal task force tackling the Drew Street clique of the Avenues gang in Glassell Park took this idea one step further. In that instance, authorities actually demolished the problem apartment building. Although Brooks and King were not personally involved with the Avenues case, it also evinced a ramped-up philosophy of spatial attack. One year later, newspapers announced that children could now play safely in the streets. In these cases, targeting domestic spaces that housed both criminal and noncriminal occupants played in direct opposition to the hallmark high precision of current antigang policing.

Paying attention to the intersection of law enforcement officials with those whom they police shows the much broader role that state violence plays in everyday life.[3] The narratives in this text frame gang neighborhoods as both violent and socially vulnerable spaces, whose shape is intimately related to state policies. We cannot understand people's experiences within those spaces without looking at how the state develops taxonomies of status, association, and guilt. Crime suppression, particularly the war on drugs, is a legal construct that paradoxically reinforces unconventional or illegal forms of cooperation among community members. In Los Angeles, gangs remain a potent challenge despite years of intrusion by law enforcement, partly because aspects of their power are the result of incarceration.

Because most theories of gang membership, policing, or neighborhood crime keep our gaze focused on an abstract neighborhood scale, they miss much with regard to the ultimate causes of crime. Broader sociopolitical and economic forces, and historic racism and segregation reach far beyond the bounds of the ghetto—and beyond the control of ghetto residents.

Most people I speak to in the neighborhoods where I work believe in Conspiracy with a capital C: that somehow the lawyer, the police officer, the sheriff's deputy, the judge, and the FBI agents are all in cahoots; that they are working through a grander directive to make their living off the black community and poor people in general; and that the greater goal is to keep people of color too disorganized to claim power in society. Although I continue to reject conspiratorial notions, they give shape to a certain feeling on the ground that I also recognize. It is the feeling that everything favors one side, that people are watching, that friends are not really friends, that life is no longer private, that you may be vulnerable to the government's blanketing enmity. As easy as criminal conspiracy is to prove in court, the Conspiracy implied in the merger of legal and illegal surveillance grids has a much more tenuous foothold. As with the 100:1 disparity, intentionality is difficult to prove.

Othering, rather than true conspiracy, is the real problem. It explains why an attorney on the ground might try to bend the law for a maximum penalty. It explains why the judge might not notice if a U.S. attorney radically shifts the standards of evidence. It explains why a sheriff's deputy might falsify evidence so that the drugs match a certain date. What authorities know and what they can prove are often two different things, and sometimes their attendant actions narrow the line between good guys and bad guys.

However successful antigang work may seem, mitigating factors compromise its long-term success. Collateral damage to families, the disorganizing removal of gang control from impoverished areas, the creation of distrust through snitching, and in particular the many incarcerated gang members who continually cycle in and out of prison will ultimately challenge whatever benefits punitive actions bring.

Law enforcement agrees that something must be put in place after a takedown like Fly Trap. Officer Anthony Rivera of the Los Angeles Gang Information Network (LARGIN) voiced a critique I heard repeatedly from law enforcement about the task force methodology:

> Once you leave, they come right back and they take over. Gangs didn't evolve in thirty days. You cannot just think you're going to go into forty years of gang membership overnight. It has to be a very long and protracted effort. To sustain it is highly expensive. Do we have the manpower? Enough funding? No. When a person points a gun, he has the almighty power of God to decide whether you are going to live or die. These people are out on the streets. We're not going to rehabilitate them. We're housing them. What are you going to do with them? We cannot treat gang members like we did in the '80s. Prison gangs are the same thing as are going on in the streets. The same stuff happens: rapes, robberies, assaults, murder. It's like taking the cancer from the street, and moving the cancer inside the jail facility. It's still a cancer.

Destroying gangs wholesale is a lofty goal but rarely a viable enterprise. In gentrifying neighborhoods with a range of economic and educational opportunities already available to residents, a few individuals or families may be responsible for both drawing and creating violence there. A task force may drive out remaining gang members in such circumstances. In more impoverished areas, however, even successful gang work may be deceiving: Brooks's disappeared 6-9 Crips, for example, have now likely made room for an existing Latino gang to monopolize the drug trade in that area, mirroring the demographic shift from black to Latino in South Central as a whole.

While law enforcement tends to narrow its focus to patterns of crime, arrest, and punishment, this book's goal has been different. It instead uses an alternative pattern that includes the contexts that inform crime and the consequences that accompany the suppression of crime. This pattern draws attention to how different social orders internal to gangs impact violence in neighborhoods. The drug trade is one, street gang politics is another, and a third is prison-level gang politics. Despite overlap among all of these, they remain semi-distinct systems that sometimes conflict with one another. Leaders in one may not be leaders in the other. By no means is a drug task force an automatic proxy for targeting gang leadership. The Fly Trap drug conspiracy netted some violent individuals and some nonviolent ones. Task forces post–Fly Trap similarly stress the membership status of both gang and nongang individuals by classifying them as gang members, gang affiliates, or shot callers.[4]

Abraham Lincoln's assertion on the stone tablet mentioned earlier that "no law is stronger than is the public sentiment where it is to be enforced" carries two interrelated meanings relevant to this project. The first is simple on its face: laws are effective only if the public supports them. The drug war's latest iteration demonstrates how lukewarm public support for the incarceration of nonviolent offenders has helped gangs to become entrenched as federal targets. Associations between gangs and violence have strengthened symbolic ties between the drug trade and violence in the same way that crack did in the mid-1980s. With hindsight, we know that connections between crack and violence proved fallacious, a circumstance of the streets rather than an automatic by-product of crack itself. The connection of gangs to explicit acts of violence is more direct. But the circumstances of the streets, the results of suppression and incarceration, and the failure to align young people with shifting economies are cut of the same cloth. Gangs, as with crack before them, are both symptom and scapegoat for greater social ills, which remain untreated by attacking them directly. Penalizing gang members as drug users or drug dealers provides an altered continuation of the drug war. Although it targets easily vilified individuals, antigang suppression incarcerates a similar class of people, as did the drug war before it: mostly young men and women of color. Gangs are quickly becoming the greatest new contributors to racial disparities within the federal system, even as the crack disparities are close to being rectified.

While public sentiment surrounding antigang legislation is waxing as opposed to waning, the fallout that results from penalizing gangs will undermine its potential success. The reason lies in a second interpretation of Lincoln's quotation. A community's values, networks, and ways of being generally provide more effective social protections than do formal legal mechanisms. To use Lincoln's words, "public sentiment" is imbued with the strength of horizontal structures and informal networks. These comprise the extralegal mechanisms of control that, when whole and strong, make both criminal justice and social justice efforts more successful. Punitive campaigns sacrifice informal control mechanisms for formal ones. Lincoln's quotation speaks to the power of social control both inside and outside of the formal legal process.

In Fly Trap, courtroom debate surrounding Lococo's wiretap evidence used a legal doctrine lyrically known as "fruit of the poison tree." Fruit of the poison tree dictates that, if evidence is obtained illegally or unjustifiably, further evidence obtained from that evidence must also be considered tainted. King based his wiretap justification largely on the fear of violence. He argued that the neighborhoods were too dangerous for informants and undercover work to be effective. Although $14,000 of the fed's money had already facilitated a key drug sale, agents argued that it wasn't enough. During the Lococo appeal, federal public defenders countered that the prosecution couldn't have it both ways. U.S. attorneys could not say one minute how successful they had been in the neighborhoods and then in the next say the neighborhoods were too dangerous for them to be successful. The Ninth Circuit Court disagreed. King's wiretap justification was upheld, creating legal precedent for similar wiretaps in similar task forces. Had the wiretap been deemed illegal, the resulting evidence have been inadmissible—fruit of the poison tree.

As a metaphor, fruit of the poison tree merits application to our society's approach to gangs, drugs, and crime as a whole. Incarceration, while licit, is nurtured on separation, community dissolution, and fear. Although widespread incarceration bears the attraction of warehousing undesirables, it also results in unintended, destructive, and sometimes invisible consequences to families and communities. Were gang sweeps part of a sparsely employed incarceration project saved for our worst offenders, were prisons rife with rehabilitative, mental health, and educational programs, were lockups instead turned into therapeutic "antiprisons" as James Gilligan proposes, then we could proceed to build stronger systems in and around them and retain incarceration as a valuable tool. But any social project that disproportionately draws resources from communities, families, and children, that takes from supportive systems such as housing, education, and health, is a social failure on the grandest scale.

William Blake's poem "A Poison Tree,"[5] upon which the legal argument is based, teaches us that anything nurtured with hate, fear, and silence is a danger, no matter how attractive its guise. This book has worked within the lessons of Blake's poem by developing narratives that run counter to incarceration's power to silence. The frustration that Assistant U.S. Attorney Jennifer Corbet felt at the voicelessness of victims is not uncommon in the judicial process. Nor is it so different from Donald Braman's conclusion that a void of silence surrounds the families of offenders, or Lorna Rhodes's assertion that a "pent-up narrative energy" exists among prison workers and the incarcerated alike.[6] Claudia in chapter 3 wondered when someone would show up to listen to her. The people with whom I conducted interviews usually lacked opportunity for public expression. The nature of our criminal justice system is to censor voices rather than to open dialogues, to create misrepresentative caricatures rather than nuanced portraits.

One of the findings of this research diverges from other work on incarceration around the country. Several authors indicate how stigma associated with prison time is partly responsible for people's isolation in already stressed communities. Shame renders people with incarcerated relatives unable to communicate openly with others and forces them to withdraw from community networks. By contrast, this project's participants live in a social milieu so scarred by incarceration that having a parent, child, relative, or friend in prison has ceased to be remarkable. Shame is a sentiment rooted in community that can work within informal networks to prevent crime. That prison no longer engenders this emotion signals a society that has gone too far. It has made radical disruptions in families and communities into normal, expected parts of life. In so doing it has effectively disempowered people from believing they can control their own circumstances.

There are problems with shame, to be sure. Shame engenders violence like no other sentiment, in addition to increasing social isolation or exclusion. Anthropologists, however, also understand that societies use shame and guilt, in appropriate doses, as tools for integration and conformity. Both the presence and absence of shame indicate a society sick from incarceration's many consequences.

With its au courant use of wiretaps, confidential informants, precise targeting, and a high conviction rate, Operation Fly Trap can be regarded as an archetypal genre of investigation. With the 2007 Bush appointment of Thomas P. O'Brien as the U.S. attorney for California's Central Division, gang-related task force investigations began to run at lightening speed, churning out investigation-to-prosecution cycles in months as opposed to years, as had been the case with Fly Trap.[7] Each task force has its own story, characters, victories, and tragedies, almost none of which become publicly known.

Mark Brooks spearheaded a follow-up 2010 sweep in the Pueblos neighborhood in which he was able to put the hard-won Fly Trap lessons into play. In Operation Family Ties, the foundational law enforcement narrative had changed. It used the numerous kin ties among targets to compare the Pueblos with the Mafia, which in turn allowed the targets to be tried under RICO, the Racketeer Influenced and Corrupt Organizations Act—the first time RICO has been used against a black gang. The charges included murder, attempted murder, and even an ugly execution in front of a two-year-old child. The use of RICO is critical in the era of post–crack reform sentencing. Operation Family Ties' comprehensive list of kin connections, which in Fly Trap disrupted media, court, and legal statements, is now a successful part of a new, post–crack reform, narrative of precision.

After Fly Trap, Special Agent King spent eighteen months in Washington, D.C., working Crimes against Children. Having to maintain a family long-distance put a massive strain on the relationship between him and his wife Lea Ann. Although they were happily reunited after that grueling period, their experience demonstrates that, no matter how lofty the cause, separation places undue pressure on relationships, on family members, and on children. When that pressure is magnified throughout a community, when it bears the stain of moral turpitude, when it is complicated by financial hardship and the ongoing hostility of punitive systems involving police, courts, child protective services, and welfare, the resulting collective breakdown is strong enough to be feared in its own right.

In the end, this project steers clear of asking who bears ultimate culpability for the violence that gangs demonstrate. It rather seeks to articulate overlapping responsibilities in the policies, circumstances, and politics that surround gang violence. I asked John Edwards's sister Renee what she thought authorities might do to help families in the wake of gang sweeps. She said, "I don't know. I don't even think they think the family exists." She thought better of it and then said, "I think they think this *is* trying to help the family." We both laughed.

The manner in which the drug war has been converted into a war on gangs constitutes a pattern of surveillance and suppression that is growing, along with the growth of gangs, worldwide. Negative outcomes taint this process. Tools of suppression may unintentionally worsen the gang problem and its violence by inadvertently strengthening gang networks, by diminishing gang control, or by making gangs impervious to punishment. Sometimes more elaborate forms of organization result from suppression; other times gangs nurture the ability to operate without formal hierarchy. After the use of spatially predictable antigang tactics, gang members seek new locations, or learn to hide their activities inside and underground, when it would be better to have them outside and above ground, where it's easier to see them. A fuller understanding of the state's role in creating violent groups like gangs requires learning the perspectives of people living in poverty and law enforcement officials alike. Presenting such perspectives together, no matter how opposed or flawed, has been my goal in this book.

As of 2011, nearly everyone convicted in the Fly Trap case has been released. In February 2011, Kevin Allen was sent to a halfway house on 94th and Central, in the neighborhood of the Nine Duse Bishops. This location was already too close to home: the Pueblo Bishops were historic allies with the Nine Duse Bishops. The Pueblos had long had a contract out on Kevin, the man once known as Bishop K-Rok and now a known snitch. On his first day back in Los Angeles, K-Rok ran into a key Pueblo indicted in a separate Fly Trap conspiracy charge. Shortly thereafter, K-Rok realized that another resident of the halfway house had been incarcerated with him at Victorville and knew about his situation. The secret K-Rok had scarcely managed to keep within the confines of the prison in Florence, Colorado, where he served his time was proving more difficult to control in residential confinement, with only a few federal facilities in any given city. K-Rok reached out to someone he knew he could trust: Mark Brooks. Brooks was able to help him request a transfer to a halfway house in El Monte, far across town from the South Central neighborhoods. "I guess we need each other," K-Rok said of Brooks. "I have respect for him. He's just trying to do his job; I'm just trying to do my job. It's just a difference in occupations, that's all."

Ms. Jackson and her daughter Carlotte developed cancer within a short time of one another, and both had to stop work to undergo treatment. Ms. Jackson's breast cancer treatment and Carlotte's treatment for thyroid cancer were successful. In 2009, Ms. Jackson lost her house of thirty years to foreclosure and underwent a scandal involving the misuse of neighborhood council funds. She was at a low point. After moving twice, she remains in supportive contact with Tina and has rented a low-income apartment near the Jungles neighborhood. She continues to be an active member of her church.

Juan Lococo is slated for release in 2015. He owes nobody anything, he says. He played the game, took what he had coming, and "never rolled on no one."

> I owe them nothing in Culiacán, I owe the FBI and the U.S. government nothing. I'm pretty sure for myself, I can live without. I can struggle. It's when I see my children struggle or my sisters struggle, or my family struggle that I get the calling. I don't know what I'm going to do if I see them struggling and I can't do anything to help them. I know the saying is going to come into my head, "Tengo mas miedo ser pobre, que estar en el cárcel o en el pantón." I'm more afraid of being poor than in jail or in the cemetery. But I have to see how things are when I come home. Maybe I will just die an old man on my porch, a retired truck driver.

In 2011, John Edwards was transferred to Terminal Island, a facility near Long Beach, much closer to his family. His sentence is now the same as Tina's, and both are slated for release in 2025. They listen daily for news of how crack law reform retroactivity might lessen their time. Junior writes, "I am doing fine under these conditions. God have bless me with a nice surrounding. Terminal Island is a very nice place to do your confinement. My family have been real supportive. Carina has been to see me, her and the kids. It is a blessing that they are there."

Whenever I talk to Tina on the phone, she says she's fine. She has no one special inside. Her attraction to other women was part of her addiction, she says—part of what she left behind when she became close to K-Rok. "I'm just trying to take every day as it comes." She saw her mother lose everything from a distance and then regain some semblance of stability. "She's in a better place now," Tina says.

On June 30, 2011, the U.S. Sentencing Commission voted unanimously to make 2010's Fair Sentencing Act retroactive. As of this writing, Tina and Junior are awaiting news as to whether they will be among approximately 12,000 federal prisoners eligible for sentence reductions. With eight years behind bars, time is both friend and enemy to Tina and Junior. I say to Junior that another year's passing is a blessing to those inside and out. Junior says to Tina to be patient, that it's a matter of time. And Tina says, to her family and friends, thank you for sticking with me.

Notes

Introduction

1. Wright, "Expanding Federal Prison Population."
2. The Gang Prevention and Abatement Act is complex. It streamlines deportation proceedings for immigrant gang members and legislates certain approaches that are already in place to a degree, including the treatment of drug dealing, if perpetrated by a gang member, as a violent crime. The Gang Prevention and Abatement Act also adds new penalties for gang affiliation, recruitment, and intimidation. This act was launched in 2007, when it stalled in the legislative process, and again in 2009, when it was referred to the Senate Committee on the Judiciary.
3. From testimony of Debra Yang, U.S. Attorney, Central District of California, on September 17, 2003, before the Senate Committee on the Judiciary.
4. Blakeslee, *Tulia.*
5. United Nations, *World Drug Report, 2005.*
6. The economic impact of deindustrialization on Los Angeles is well summarized in Wolch, "From Global to Local."
7. Mauer, *Race to Incarcerate.*
8. R. Gilmore, *Golden Gulag.*
9. Currie, *Crime and Punishment in America*, 27.
10. Wright, "Expanding Federal Prison Population."
11. C. Gilmore, "California's Hinterlands."
12. Wright, "Expanding Federal Prison Population."
13. For an excellent analysis, see Clear, "The Problem of 'Addition by Subtraction.'"
14. For in-depth accounts of the war on gangs, see Davis, "Hammer and the Rock," chap. 5 of *City of Quartz*, and Hayden, *Street Wars.*
15. Gang suppression policies have sometimes forced gangs to become more decentralized and underground entities, a paradoxical yet predictable trend that has also occurred internationally. Policies including deportation, enhancements,

and injunctions have had unintended effects that strengthen certain elements of gang membership. Gang deportations, for example, have generated long-feared international connections between gang members in the United States and Central America. See Hayden, *Street Wars,* and Zilberg, *Space of Detention.*

16. Although suppression seems a logical follow-up to higher rates of neighborhood violence, the history of antigang work emphasizes the variable relationship of gang suppression to rates of crime. Gang sweeps have sometimes been instituted during lows in violence and not just during crisis periods. Enhanced suppression may accompany gentrification projects or high-profile media stories as opposed to crisis-level violence on the ground. Hayden, *Street Wars,* and Moore, *Going Down to the Barrio.*

17. Davis, "Hammer and the Rock," chap. 5 of *City of Quartz.*

18. Ties between pachucos and anarchist or fascist groups were soon debunked as Hearstian yellow journalism. See Mazon, *Zoot Suit Riots,* for an excellent account of the pachuco era and its attendant publicity. In terms of early FBI history in Los Angeles, Hollywood star extortions, Mexican revolutionary activity, Japanese spy cases, and the work of political subversives were FBI staples well into the 1960s.

19. FBI, "Fighting Gang Violence" (statistics on gangs).

20. FBI, "Arrests Made in Joint Operation Fly Trap Targeting Violent Los Angeles Street Gangs," press release, June 26, 2003.

21. Buntin, "Gangbuster."

22. James Q. Wilson and George L. Kelling first defined the broken windows theory in a 1982 *Atlantic Monthly* article, "Broken Windows," that identified a link between crime rates and a neighborhood's material conditions. Studies both support and detract from the theory, and oftentimes its implementation or testing looks very different from the concepts laid out in the original article.

23. Jeralyn, "LA Chief Bill Bratton Puts 'Broken Window' Policing into Action."

24. Part of the problem with applying the broken windows theory is that almost any crime can qualify as a broken window, depending on the context. Whereas the original theory attempted to assess the relationship of material conditions to crime, the theory now assumes that "smaller" crimes lead to "bigger" crimes. This assumption makes the argument less precise. The main problems with countertheory collective efficacy, by contrast, are that some assumption of community uniformity informs the theory and that the class-specific dimensions of the theory are underdeveloped. Both theories suffer from the lack of any in-depth associated ethnography of people's lives on the ground, or their perceptions of crime or policing—something the original broken windows theorists were right to be interested in.

25. Hayden, *Street Wars.*

26. Arjun Appadurai observes that cellular, interconnected networks that espouse violence as a core principle oppose but also mirror certain aspects of global markets: "So there is a double sense of nausea and uncertainty that these networks

produce. They seek to reverse the relationship between peace and everyday life, and they do so without any regard for those principles of vertebrate coordination on which the nation-state has always relied. This is an epistemological assault on us all, for it destabilizes our two most cherished assumptions—that peace is the natural marker of social order and that the nation-state is the natural guarantor and container of such order." Appadurai, *Fear of Small Numbers*, 32–33.

27. Scholarship in this area deals often with externalized political violence such as interethnic violence, ethnic cleansing, genocide, or terrorist attacks. Overlap between highly politicized violence projects and the internalized violence of gangs requires greater theoretical and ethnographic exploration. See Hagedorn, *Gangs in the Global City*; Brotherton and Venkatesh, *Globalization, Youth Violence, and the Law*; also Biehl, *Vita*. See also Das et al., introduction to *Violence and Subjectivity*.

28. Wacquant, "Decivilizing and Demonizing," 95.

29. Vigil, *Projects*, 200.

30. Venkatesh, *Gang Leader for a Day*; Hagedorn, *Gangs in the Global City*.

31. Tocqueville, *Democracy in America*, 198–200.

32. Pew Center on the States, *One in 100*.

33. Mauer argues, "Most criminal justice officials now recognize that prison populations represent public policy choices as much as they do crime rates." Mauer, "Crisis of the Young African American Male," 14.

34. See, for example, Glassner, *Culture of Fear,* or Macek, *Urban Nightmares,* for treatments of the generative relationship between media and crime.

35. See Rhodes, *Total Confinement,* and Singer, *Drugging the Poor*, or Reinarman and Levine, *Crack in America*. They write: "the inner-city poor and working class are far less often employed and more often live at the margins of the conventional order. When their lives become too difficult, they rarely have psychiatrists, but they sometimes self-medicate, escape, or seek moments of intense euphoria with what might be called antidespondents, such as crack. When some of them become addicted, they have far fewer resources to use to pull themselves out of trouble and far fewer opportunities to make a successful life.... And when some of the inner-city poor began having trouble with crack, politicians declared a drug war that did not help them stabilize their lives." Reinarman and Levine, *Crack in America*, 13.

36. The popular Stop Snitchin', Stop Lyin' movement began in Baltimore in 2004 and has spread rapidly around the country through street venues to critique the social costs of snitching. The movement is controversial, and its Stop Snitchin' T-shirts have been banned in several East Coast courthouses as a form of witness intimidation. See Hampson, "Anti-Snitch Campaign Riles Police, Prosecutors," and Natapoff, "Bait and Snitch."

37. Marx, *Undercover*. See also Laura Nader's argument regarding white-collar crime in Nader, "Crime as a Category, Domestic and Globalized."

38. Hayden, *Street Wars*.

39. The federal sentencing guidelines may be found on the website of the U.S. Sentencing Commission, http://www.ussc.gov/Guidelines/2010_guidelines/index .cfm.

CHAPTER 1. The Game

1. Most cartel heads are from Sinaloa no matter which cartel they belong to or which area they control.

2. Parson, *Making a Better World*. See in particular chap. 2, "Homes for Heroes: Public Housing during WWII."

3. Thirteen-year-old Gilberto Reynaga was killed on his way home by a Blue Line train as he attempted to hop through two parked freight cars. The Blue Line is the MTA light rail line that has claimed more lives than any other in Los Angeles in a twelve-mile stretch, where it is legally allowed to run through urban neighborhoods at 55 mph. See Shuit, "85% of Blue Line Deaths Occur on Fastest Segment."

4. Gang spelling of the word "deuce" varies according to whether the gang is affiliated with Bloods or Crips. Because the Pueblo Bishops are Bloods, they generally avoid the *c* and spell "deuce" with an *s*, as "duse." Crip gangs tend to spell "deuce" with a *c*, as "duce." Both Bloods and Crips sometimes spell the word traditionally and, if appropriate, will cross out the *c* associated with that word.

5. Absolution or underpunishment of snitches for their crimes is one reason why they are linked with the continuation if not the rise of crime in low-income neighborhoods. Because higher-level criminals often have more information, often times they walk away with absurdly light sentences, whereas lesser involved, ill-informed partners or subservients (girlfriends, mothers, workers, etc.) bear the full force of the sentencing laws.

6. Natapoff, "Snitching: Consequences," 646. Natapoff writes, "using criminal informants exacerbates some of the worst features of the U.S. justice system. The practice is clandestine and unregulated, inviting inaccuracy, crime, and sometimes corruption. It inflicts special harms on vulnerable individuals such as racial minorities, substance abusers, and poor defendants who lack robust legal representation. Because of its secretive and discretionary nature, it evades the traditional checks and balances of judicial and public scrutiny, even as it determines the outcomes of millions of investigations and cases. And finally, like the criminal justice system itself, it is rapidly expanding." Natapoff, *Snitching: Criminal Informants*, 3.

7. Lococo's suspicions were incorrect in this case. FBI paperwork identified CS-2 as a member of the Pueblo Bishops gang; CS-3 and CS-4 were in custody and members of the 38th Street gang. Only CS-1 had information about Edwards and Jackson.

8. Thanks to a longtime federal inmate and anonymous friend for the e-mail exchange that led to this list. The feminizing construction of snitching terms is part of the reason it plays into hypermasculinist violence in response.

9. Electronic Privacy Information Center, "Title III Electronic Surveillance."

10. *Lethal Weapon* was a 1987 action comedy movie starring Danny Glover and Mel Gibson.

CHAPTER 2. **Charlotte's Web**

1. See, for example, Nepomnaschy et al., "Cortisol Level and Very Early Pregnancy Loss in Humans," an article that discusses links between miscarriage and stress.

2. King affidavit, 3, of complaint for violations of Title 21, U.S.C. §846, United States v. Anthony Lamont Deal, Juan Emanuel Lococo, Charlotte Venia Jackson, and Deborah Wimberly, magistrates case 03-139 3M (Magistrate Judge Paul Game, Jr.).

3. See Sekula, "Traffic in Photographs," for a seminal article that analyzes mug shots and the history of police photography.

4. "Arrests Made in Joint Operation Fly Trap Targeting Violent Los Angeles Street Gangs," press release, FBI, June 26, 2003.

5. Feldman, "Violence and Vision."

6. The sociological debate about the nature of underclass is based on the same categorizations. Wacquant reminds us that the term "underclass" is defined by deficiency and middle-class standards, and excludes the historicity of the ghetto as an exclusionary project. See Wacquant, "Three Pernicious Premises in the Study of the American Ghetto."

7. County of Los Angeles Sheriff's Department, incident report 403-00749-3440-181, p. 5.

8. This falsification was used as a successful plea bargaining tool that reduced what could have been a twenty-five year sentence to only three years. The state of California is considering legislation that will require law enforcement to tape all interrogations and the courts to warn juries that unrecorded accounts of interrogations may not be reliable. This is not because all officers or criminals are immoral or liars. Anna Tsing argues in *Friction* that even the accounts of people on the same side of an issue can differ wildly. Here, the power of othering to shape the two narratives into opposing views tells more than splitting hairs about the veracity of either account.

9. FBI, FD-302, file 166E-LA-228163-302-312, by Special Agent Jose Moreno, June 1, 2003.

10. U.S. Department of Justice, "Los Angeles Men Sentenced in Gang-Related Crack Cocaine Trafficking Case," press release, July 13, 2005, http://www.justice.gov/usao/cac/pressroom/pr2005/102html.

11. See *U.S. v. Deal, Lococo, Jackson, and Wimberly*, at 11–14. Gang membership section begins on p. 10.

12. Juan Lococo lived in the 38th Street neighborhood, but only his brother was a member of that gang.

13. Baker, *Blues, Ideology, and Afro-American Literature.*

14. Even a single person has trouble surviving and paying rent on a minimum wage job; supplementing a stable income through collective enterprise, and further through the stability of something such as the drug trade, becomes critical for family survival. Those who receive welfare benefits face similar challenges. Several studies argue that, because welfare benefits never provide enough to support families in full, welfare rates can be used as a proxy to gauge the size of the informal economy. See Ehrenreich, *Nickel and Dimed;* Edin and Lein, *Making Ends Meet;* Newman, *No Shame in My Game;* and Bourgois, *In Search of Respect.*

15. John Russo and Sherry Lee Linkon write: "Although the relationship between persistently high unemployment and per capita murder rates is well established, it was rarely discussed in the local media. The [local newspaper] compared Youngstown with Gary, Indiana and Compton, California, whose murder rates were often higher, without mentioning that both of those cities had also experienced high levels of unemployment and deindustrialization.... Deindustrialization exacted enormous social and economic costs, and the rising crime rate was one of those costs." Russo and Linkon, *Steeltown USA,* 211.

16. One could argue that the earlier list of kin ties simply list re-pathologizes black families by framing an extended kin network through criminality in the same way as the task force did. This critique is partly true, because not all kin ties within that same community are linked to criminality. The problem, however, is how many aspects of these neighborhoods nevertheless are touched by criminality. The persistently localized focus of crime suppression has taken an enormous toll on noncriminals within this extended network of individuals, and I discuss some of the ramifications in chapter 3.

CHAPTER 3. Broken Families

1. Yablonsky, *Fathers and Sons.*

2. *United States v. Aguirre,* 214 F. 3d 1122, 9th Cir., 2000.

3. I was unable to contact several of the Fly Trap targets, and the other twenty-one remained unconvinced of my motives and the project's veracity. Another factor limiting participation included my inability to find persons whose names were on the original list but who were never charged, those who were released before research began, and those in the state as opposed to the federal system; another limiting factor was working with those with literacy issues, in a methodology dependent on writing letters.

4. This family was hesitant to participate in this project. As a result of close ties among people in the case, I found out about the many kin ties to this boy and the consequences of his death for the Fly Trap network.

5. See, for example, Farmer, "House of the Dead," or Gaes and Kendig, "Skill Sets and Health Care Needs of Released Offenders."

6. This finding runs opposite to those on spousal loss, in which elderly men make up the majority of deaths because they generally have not been the center of constructing family life.

7. Wacquant, "Decivilizing and Demonizing," 115.

8. Beth E. Richie says: "the already overburdened role of caretaker in low-income families is further complicated by the constant threat women face of possible arrest and detention of a family member, chaotic trials, long prison sentences, parole hearings, probation requirements that may involve making a change in household arrangements if more than one family member has a felony conviction, and the ever-present risk of rearrest ... [and the attention of] the state's child protection apparatus." Richie, "Social Impact of Mass Incarceration on Women," 146.

9. Far from perks, commissary items are critical for a prisoner's health and well-being. They are also a locus of significant corporate exploitation.

10. Donald Braman argues a "negative potential of sharing burdens and benefits" in communities with high incarceration rates. He says, "the rise of incarceration has not simply punished criminal offenders; it has disrupted and impoverished their families and communities as well. Thus, as incarceration rates have burgeoned over the last generation, so too have the costs to all of those in traditional networks of exchange and mutual aid. The result is that the relationships and norms described as social capital have increasingly become burdens rather than benefits to many inner-city families. This is no minor concern. These networks are the life-blood of a healthy society, and their erosion is not just material but deeply social." Braman, *Doing Time on the Outside*, 7.

11. Pew Center on the States, *One in 100*.

12. Ms. Jackson was referring to the day the judge sentenced Tawana to eight years.

13. Ms. Jackson's son, Clifford, was also named in the list of twenty-eight, but his charges were never filed. He had been a street addict and likely played a low-level role in the conspiracy, meriting his inclusion on the list but not a formal charge.

14. Braman, "Social Silence," chap. 18 of *Doing Time on the Outside*.

15. For example, the "declining number of marriageable men in the African American community" and "high rates of homicide, AIDS-related deaths and other factors" have "created a substantial imbalance in the male-female ratio among adult African Americans ... by the age range 40–44, [gender ratios decline] to 86 males per 100 females." Whites remain 100:100 for this group. Mauer, "Crisis of the Young African American Male," 12.

16. See, for example, Tucker and Mitchell-Kernan, *Decline in Marriage among African Americans*; Bennett, Bloom, and Craig, "Divergence of Black and White Marriage Patterns."

CHAPTER 4. **Cutting the Head off the Snake**

1. Reich, "Stray Gunfire Kills Woman."

2. Schwartz, "Remembering Victim, Mourners Vow to Seek Peace."

3. The drug trade is part of what holds back full-blown warfare between black and Latino gangs. Black gangs buy their drugs from Latino gangs, in part fueling the Mexican Mafia's profits. Should Latino gangs manage to drive away African American gangs from shared neighborhood spaces, however, the Mexican Mafia's profit margins would increase even further. Racialized animosity as well as long-standing alliance between certain black and Latino gangs continue despite widespread, Mexican Mafia–endorsed cleansing campaigns against African Americans.

4. Historic exceptions to this rule may be found in majority-Bloods cities, such as Inglewood, or certain places in California's Bay Area.

5. Cintron, "Listening to What the Streets Say."

6. LAPD Online, "Compstat Policing in Los Angeles."

7. A third idea points to potential changes in police reporting of gang crime that might have taken place after the sweep. This possibility brings up the need for in-depth study of police behavior before and after major suppression events.

8. A classic text on this national issue is Maxson and Klein, "Street Gang Violence."

9. Another problem with LAPD statistics is how to calculate the number of gang members in the city. For Los Angeles, numbers declined in the years between 1996 and 2006, from around 60,000 to 40,000. While numbers during some years in this period remain stable in terms of population, some months exhibit drops of thousands of individuals. For example, in the span of just one month from November 2004 to December 2004, the gang population of Los Angeles declined by 6,123 individuals. Counting problems are severe, so the numbers can be manipulated by politicians or others who wish to use them rhetorically.

10. Gilligan, *Preventing Violence,* and Clear, "Problem with 'Addition by Subtraction.'"

11. This version of the story is based on Brooks's recounting of these events. Brooks later argued that "the community says what they want to say to make them seem right."

12. Fortes and Evans-Prichard, in *African Political Systems,* term this style of political organization a "type B." Appadurai uses the term "cellular" in his 2006 treatment of terrorism, *Fear of Small Numbers.* Deleuze and Guattari spend a great deal of time with "rhizomatic" structure and segmentation in their 1987 *Thousand Plateaus.* Scott writes of "escape social structure" in his 2009 *Art of Not Being Governed.*

13. BBC News, "Divided by Bars and Colour."

14. A related argument can be made with regard to law enforcement, wherein some "problem" officers have a useful place. Throughout the war on gangs, officers

with aggressive personalities were frequent recruits to specialized antigang units during the CRASH (Community Resources against Street Hoodlums) era of the LAPD. Indeed, the frequency of their out-of-control behavior ultimately became part of the reason the units were disbanded.

15. Levitt and Venkatesh, "Economic Analysis of a Drug-Selling Gang's Finances," 758.

CHAPTER 5. The Prosecutor's Darling

1. Emerson, *System of Freedom of Expression*, as quoted in Abbate, "Conspiracy Doctrine," 296.

2. United States v. Stoner, 98 F.3d 527, 533 (10th Cir. 1996), as quoted in Casey and Marino, *Federal Criminal Conspiracy*, 578–79.

3. Abbate, "Conspiracy Doctrine," 297.

4. Darrow, *Story of My Life*, 64.

5. See Merrill Singer's three-part series on licit and illicit drug use and production, in particular *Drugging the Poor*.

6. Glaze and James, *Mental Health Problems of Prison and Jail Inmates*, 4.

7. See Fakhoury and Priebe, "Deinstitutionalization and Reinstitutionalization," and Stroman, *Disability Rights Movement*, for reviews of deinstitutionalization and its impact in the United States.

8. Human Rights Watch, *Ill-Equipped*.

9. Clear, *Imprisoning Communities*, 52.

10. King and Mauer, "Sentencing with Discretion."

11. Leadership Conference on Civil Rights Education Fund, *Bush Administration Takes Aim*, 22.

12. American Civil Liberties Union, *Interested Persons Memo on Crack/Powder Cocaine Sentencing Policy*, iii.

13. Taifa, "Racial Disparities in the U.S. Criminal Justice System," 7.

14. Abbate, "Conspiracy Doctrine," 310.

15. United States v. P. McGuire, 307 F.3d 1192 (9th Cir. 2002).

16. See, for example, Nader, "Crime as a Category."

17. This fact continued to rankle Lococo and eventually formed a successful basis for his appeal.

18. Sentencing memorandum, Government's Consolidated Objections and Position re: Presentence Reports for Defendants John D. Edwards, Juan Lococo, and Charlotte Jackson, and Declaration of Mark Brooks, submitted by Kevin S. Rosenberg, United States v. John D. Edwards, Juan Emanuel Lococo, and Charlotte Venia Jackson, nos. CR 03-687-RKG and CR 03-689-RKG, pp. 7–8.

19. The range depends on criminal history, acceptance of responsibility, use of a minor, leadership role, and any information provided that assists courts or police.

20. Sentencing memorandum, *U.S. v. Edwards, Lococo, and Jackson*, at 21.

21. Reinarman and Levine, *Crack in America*.

22. In the late 1990s, criminologist Todd Clear and other researchers conducted a study of prison inmates' perspectives on religion. They found that existing beliefs, internal conflicts, legal status, and prison survival shape an inmate's religious practice. Some inmates, they say, continually resist their sentences and blame others for their situation. "But for some inmates, there can be no denying. For these, the attack against the self, represented by the prison term, is too real to be denied. A certain truth about their lives must be confronted: the final failure of their choices. Religion, in its substance, holds possible routes out of the dilemma, for it not only explains the cause of the failure, it also prescribes the solution." Clear et al., "Value of Religion in Prison," 57–58.

CONCLUSION: **Fruit of the Poison Tree**

1. The two statues are by two different sculptors. The woman, *Law*, is of sandstone and was carved in 1940–41 by Archibald Garner. The man, *The Young Lincoln*, is of limestone and was carved in 1938–41 by James Lee Hansen. Both are examples of New Deal public art.

2. *Molecule Man*, created by Jonathan Borofsky in 1991.

3. Here I'm thinking in particular of the work of Philippe Bourgois, James Gilligan, and Nancy Scheper-Hughes. See, for example, Bourgois, "Power of Violence in War and Peace," Gilligan, *Preventing Violence*, and Scheper-Hughes, "Small Wars and Invisible Genocides."

4. The use of "shot caller" as a rhetorical term is so overused it has become nearly meaningless as a specific concept, even while it continues to gain popularity in court and media presentations.

5. See Blake, "A Poison Tree," in *Songs of Innocence, Songs of Experience*.

6. Braman, *Doing Time on the Outside*, and Rhodes, *Total Confinement*, xi.

7. John R. Emshwiller, "Federal Law Enforcement."

Bibliography

Abbate, Fred J. "The Conspiracy Doctrine: A Critique." *Philosophy and Public Affairs* 3, no. 3 (1974): 295–311.

Advancement Project. *A Call to Action: A Case for a Comprehensive Solution to LA's Gang Violence Epidemic.* Los Angeles and Washington, DC: Advancement Project, 2008.

American Civil Liberties Union. *Interested Persons Memo on Crack/Powder Cocaine Sentencing Policy.* 2002. http://www.aclu.org/drugpolicy/sentencing/10662leg20020521.html#_ednref1.

Appadurai, Arjun. *Fear of Small Numbers: An Essay on the Geography of Anger.* Durham, NC: Duke University Press, 2006.

Baker, Houston A., Jr. *Blues, Ideology, and Afro-American Literature: A Vernacular Theory.* Chicago: University of Chicago Press, 1984.

BBC News. "Divided by Bars and Colour: Federal Prosecutors in the United States Say They Have Smashed the Country's Most Powerful Whites-Only Prison Gang." *BBC News Online*, December 5, 2002. http://news.bbc.co.uk/1/low/world/americas/2447403.stm.

Bennett, Neil G., David E. Bloom, and Patricia H. Craig, P. H. "The Divergence of Black and White Marriage Patterns." *American Journal of Sociology* 95, no. 3 (1989): 692–722.

Biehl, João. *Vita: Life in a Zone of Social Abandonment.* Berkeley: University of California Press, 2005.

Blake, William. *Songs of Innocence and Songs of Experience: The Classic Poetry of William Blake.* Rockville, MD: Wildside Press, 2009.

Blakeslee, Nate. *Tulia: Race, Cocaine, and Corruption in a Small Texas Town.* New York: Public Affairs, 2005.

Bourgois, Philippe. *In Search of Respect: Selling Crack in el Barrio.* Cambridge: Cambridge University Press, 1998.

———. "The Power of Violence in War and Peace: Post–Cold War Lessons from El Salvador." *Ethnography* 2, no. 1 (2001): 5–37.

Braman, Donald. *Doing Time on the Outside: Incarceration and Family Life in Urban America*. Ann Arbor: University of Michigan Press, 2004.

Brotherton, David, and Sudhir Venkatesh. *Globalization, Youth Violence, and the Law*. Stanford: Stanford University Press, 2007.

Bullard, Robert. "Differential Vulnerabilities: Environmental and Economic Inequality and Government Response to Unnatural Disasters." *Social Research: An International Quarterly* 75, no. 3 (2008): 753–84.

Buntin, John. "Gangbuster." December 2003. http://www.governing.com/topics/public-justics-safety/A-Gangbuster.html.

Casey, Carrie, and Marino, Lisa. "Federal Criminal Conspiracy." *American Criminal Law Review* 40 (2003): 577–612.

Cintron, Ralph. "Listening to What the Streets Say: Vengeance as Ideology?" *Annals of the American Academy of Political and Social Science* 567, no. 1 (2000): 42–53.

Clear, Todd R. *Imprisoning Communities: How Mass Incarceration Makes Disadvantaged Neighborhoods Worse*. Oxford: Oxford University Press, 2007.

———. "The Problem with 'Addition by Subtraction': The Prison–Crime Relationship in Low Income Communities." In *Invisible Punishment: The Collateral Consequences of Mass Imprisonment*, edited by Marc Mauer and Meda Chesney-Lind, 181–94. New York: New Press, 2003.

Clear, Todd R., Patricia L Hardyman, Bruce Stout, Karol Lucken, and Harry R. Dammer. "The Value of Religion in Prison: An Inmate Perspective." *Journal of Contemporary Criminal Justice* 16, no. 1 (2000): 53–74.

Currie, Elliott. *Crime and Punishment in America: Why the Solutions to America's Most Stubborn Social Crisis Have Not Worked—and What Will*. New York: Metropolitan Books, 1998.

Darrow, Clarence. 1996. *The Story of My Life*. With a new introduction by Alan Dershowitz. New York: Da Capo Press.

Das, Veena, Arthur Kleinman, Mamphela Ramphele, and Pamela Reynolds. *Violence and Subjectivity*. Berkeley: University of California Press, 2000.

Davis, Mike. *City of Quartz: Excavating the Future in Los Angeles*. London: Verso, 1990.

Deleuze, Gilles, and Pierre-Félix Guattari. *A Thousand Plateaus: Capitalism and Schizophrenia*. Minneapolis: University of Minnesota Press, 1987.

Edin, Kathryn, and Laura Lein. *Making Ends Meet: How Single Mothers Survive Welfare*. Thousand Oaks, CA: Russell Sage Foundation, 1997.

Ehrenreich, Barbara. *Nickel and Dimed: On (Not) Getting by in America*. New York: Henry Holt, 2008.

Electronic Privacy Information Center. "Title III Electronic Surveillance, 1968–2009." http://epic.org/privacy/wiretap/stats/wiretap_stats.html.

Emerson, Thomas I. *The System of Freedom of Expression*. New York: Vintage Books, 1970.

Emshwiller, John R. "Federal Law Enforcement Helps to Tackle Expanding Gang Problem." *Los Angeles Times*, October 16, 2008.

Fakhoury, Walid, and Stefan Priebe. "Deinstitutionalization and Reinstitutionalization: Major Changes in the Provision of Mental Healthcare." *Psychiatry* 6, no. 8 (2007): 313–16.

Farmer, Paul. "House of the Dead: Tuberculosis and Incarceration." In *Invisible Punishment: The Collateral Consequences of Mass Imprisonment*, edited by Marc Mauer and Meda Chesney-Lind, 239–57. New York: New Press, 2003.

Federal Bureau of Investigation (FBI). "Fighting Gang Violence." Recent statistics on gangs. Washington, DC, 2011. http://www.fbi.gov/about-us/investigate/vc_majorthefts/gangs/recent-statistics.

Feldman, Allen, "Violence and Vision: The Prosthetics and Aesthetics of Terror." *Public Culture* 10 (1997): 24–60.

Fitzpatrick, Tanya R. "Bereavement Events among Elderly Men: The Effects of Stress and Health." *Journal of Applied Gerontology* 17 (1998): 204–28.

Fortes, Meyer, and E. E. Evans-Prichard, eds. *African Political Systems.* London: Oxford University Press, 1940.

Gaes, Gerald G., and Newton Kendig. "The Skill Sets and Health Care Needs of Released Offenders." In *Prisoners Once Removed: The Impact of Incarceration and Reentry on Children, Families, and Communities*, edited by Jeremy Travis and Michelle Waul, 105–53. Washington, DC: Urban Institute Press, 2004.

Gilligan, James. *Preventing Violence.* London: Thames and Hudson, 2001.

Gilmore, Craig, in conversation with Trevor Paglen. "California's Hinterlands." *Recording Carceral Landscapes.* http://www.paglen.com/carceral/interview_craig_gilmore.htm.

Gilmore, Ruth. *Golden Gulag: Prisons, Surplus, Crisis, and Opposition in Globalizing California.* Berkeley: University of California Press, 2007.

Glassner, Barry. *The Culture of Fear: Why Americans Are Afraid of the Wrong Things.* New York: Basic Books, 2000.

Glaze, Lauren E., and Doris J. James. *Mental Health Problems of Prison and Jail Inmates.* Bureau of Justice Statistics special report NCJ 213600. September 2006.

Green, Judith, and Kevin Pranis. *Gang Wars: The Failure of Enforcement Tactics and the Need for Effective Public Safety Strategies.* Washington, DC: Justice Policy Institute, 2007.

Hagedorn, John, ed. *Gangs in the Global City: Alternatives to Traditional Criminology.* Urbana: University of Illinois Press, 2007.

Hampson, Rick. "Anti-Snitch Campaign Riles Police, Prosecutors." *USA Today*, March 28, 2006. http://www.usatoday.com/news/nation/2006-03-28-stop-snitching_x.htm.

Hayden, Tom. *Street Wars: Gangs and the Future of Violence in Los Angeles.* New York: New Press, 2004.

Human Rights Watch. *Ill-Equipped: U.S. Prisons and Offenders with Mental Illness.* New York: Human Rights Watch, 2003. http://www.hrw.org/en/reports/2003/10/ 21/ill-equipped.

Jeralyn. "LA Chief Bill Bratton Puts 'Broken Window' Policing into Action." *Talk Left: The Politics of Crime,* February 2, 2003. http://www.talkleft.com/story/ 2003/02/02/081/73183.

Kennedy, David. "Drugs, Race, and Common Ground: Reflections on the High Point Intervention." *National Institute of Justice Journal* 262 (2008): 12–17.

King, Ryan S., and Marc Mauer. *Sentencing with Discretion: Crack Cocaine Sentencing after Booker.* Washington, DC: Sentencing Project, 2006.

Klein, Malcolm. *The American Street Gang: Its Nature, Prevalence, and Control.* Oxford: Oxford University Press, 1995.

LAPD Online. "Compstat Policing in Los Angeles." http://www.lapdonline.org/ crime_maps_and_compstat/content_basic_view/6363. Retrieved on March 26, 2008.

———. "Gang Statistics by Month." http://www.lapdonline.org/get_informed/ content_basic_view/24435.

Leadership Conference on Civil Rights Education Fund. *The Bush Administration Takes Aim: Civil Rights under Attack.* Washington, DC: Leadership Conference on Civil Rights Education Fund, 2003.

Levitt, Steven D., and Sudhir Venkatesh. "An Economic Analysis of a Drug-Selling Gang's Finances." *Quarterly Journal of Economics* 1125, no. 3 (2000): 755–89.

Marx, Gary T. *Undercover: Police Surveillance in America.* Berkeley: University of California Press, 1988.

Macek, Steve. *Urban Nightmares: The Media, the Right, and the Moral Panic over the City.* Minneapolis: University of Minnesota Press, 2006.

Mauer, Marc. "The Crisis of the Young African American Male and the Criminal Justice System." Prepared for the U.S. Commission on Human Rights, April 15–16, 1999.

———. *Race to Incarcerate.* New York: New Press, 1999.

Mazon, Mauricio. *The Zoot Suit Riots: The Psychology of Symbolic Annihilation.* Austin: University of Texas Press, 1988.

Maxson, Cheryl, and Malcolm Klein. "Street Gang Violence: Twice as Great or Half as Great?" In *Gangs in America,* edited by C. Ronald Huff. Newbury Park, CA: Sage, 1990.

Moore, Joan. *Going Down to the Barrio: Homeboys and Homegirls in Change.* Philadelphia: Temple University Press, 1991.

Nader, Laura. "Crime as a Category, Domestic and Globalized." In *Crime's Power: Anthropologists and the Ethnography of Crime,* edited by Philip Parnell and Stephanie Kane, 55–76. New York: Palgrave Macmillan, 2003.

Natapoff, Alexandra. "Bait and Snitch: The High Cost of Snitching for Law Enforcement." *Slate Magazine Online,* December 12, 2005. http://www.slate.com/ id/2132092/.

———. *Snitching: Criminal Informants and the Erosion of American Justice.* New York: New York University Press, 2009.

———. "Snitching: The Institutional and Communal Consequences." *University of Cincinnati Law Review* 73 (2004): 645–703.

Nepomnaschy, Pablo A., Kathleen B. Welch, Daniel S. McConnell, and Barry G. England. "Cortisol Levels and Very Early Pregnancy Loss in Humans." *Proceedings of the National Academy of Sciences* 103, no. 10 (2006): 3938–42."

Newman, Katherine S. *No Shame in My Game: The Working Poor in the Inner City.* New York: Vintage. 2000.

Parenti, Christian. *Lockdown America: Police and Prisons in the Age of Crisis.* New York: Verso, 1999.

Parson, Donald Craig. *Making a Better World: Public Housing, the Red Scare, and the Direction of Modern Los Angeles.* Minneapolis: University of Minnesota Press, 2005.

Pew Center on the States. *One in 100: Behind Bars in America, 2008.* Washington, DC: Pew Center on the States' Public Safety Performance Project, 2008.

Pulido, Laura. "Rethinking Environmental Racism: White Privilege and Urban Development in Southern California." *Annals of the Association of American Geographers* 90, no. 1 (2000): 12–40.

Reich, Kenneth. "Stray Gunfire Kills Woman as 9 Bullets Strike Her Home." *Los Angeles Times*, August 7, 2001.

Reinarman, Craig, and Harry Levine, eds. *Crack in America: Demon Drugs and Social Justice.* Berkeley: University of California Press, 1997.

Rhodes, Lorna. "Taxonomic Anxieties: Axis I and Axis II." *Medical Anthropology Quarterly* 14, no. 3 (2000): 346–73.

———. *Total Confinement: Madness and Reason in the Maximum Security Prison.* Berkeley: University of California Press, 2004.

Richie, Beth E. "The Social Impact of Mass Incarceration on Women." In *Invisible Punishment: The Collateral Consequences of Mass Imprisonment,* edited by Marc Mauer and Meda Chesney-Lind, 136–49. New York: New Press, 2003.

Russo, John, and Sherry Lee Linkon, eds. *New Working-Class Studies.* Ithaca: Cornell University Press, 2005.s

———, eds. *Steeltown USA: Work and Memory in Youngstown.* Lawrence: University Press of Kansas, 2002.

Scheper-Hughes, Nancy. "Small Wars and Invisible Genocides." *Social Science and Medicine* 43, no. 5 (1966): 889–900.

Schwartz, Noaki. "In Remembering Victim, Mourners Vow to Seek Peace." *Los Angeles Times*, August 12, 2001.

Scott, James C. *The Art of Not Being Governed: An Anarchist History of Upland Southeast Asia.* New Haven: Yale University Press, 2009.

Sekula, Allan. "The Traffic in Photographs." *Art Journal* 41, no. 1 (1981): 15–25.

Shuit, Douglas P. "85% of Blue Line Deaths Occur on Fastest Segment." *Los Angeles Times*, December 23, 1999.

Singer, Merrill. *Drugging the Poor: Legal and Illegal Drugs and Social Inequality.* Long Grove, IL: Waveland Press, 2008.

Stroman, Duane. *The Disability Rights Movement: From Deinstitutionalization to Self-determination.* Lanham, MD: University Press of America, 2003.

Taifa, Nkechi. "Racial Disparities in the U.S. Criminal Justice System: Can the International Race Convention Provide a Basis for Relief?" Statement of Nkechi Taifa before the Justice Kennedy Commission, American Bar Association, November 14, 2003.

Tita, George, J. K. Riley, Greg Ridgeway, Clifford Grammich, Allan F. Abrahamse, and Peter Greenwood. *Reducing Gun Violence: Results from an Intervention in East Los Angeles.* Santa Monica, CA: RAND Press, 2003.

Tocqueville, Alexis de. *Democracy in America.* New York: Vintage Books, 1954.

Travis, Jeremy, and Michelle Waul. *Prisoners Once Removed: The Impact of Incarceration and Reentry on Children, Families, and Communities.* Washington, DC: Urban Institute Press, 2004.

Tsing, Anna. *Friction: An Ethnography of Global Connection.* Princeton: Princeton University Press, 2004.

Tucker, M. Belinda, and Claudia Mitchell-Kernan, eds. *The Decline in Marriage among African Americans: Causes, Consequences, and Policy Implications.* New York: Russell Sage Foundation, 1995.

United Nations. *World Drug Report, 2005.* Geneva: United Nations Office on Drugs and Crime, 2005.

U.S. Sentencing Commission. *2010 Federal Sentencing Guidelines Manual.* http://www.ussc.gov/Guidelines/2010_guidelines/index.cfm.

Venkatesh, Sudhir. *Gang Leader for a Day: A Rogue Sociologist Takes to the Streets.* New York: Penguin Press, 2008.

Vigil, Diego. *The Projects: Gang and Non-Gang Families in East Los Angeles.* Austin: University of Texas Press, 2007.

Wacquant, Loïc. "Decivilizing and Demonizing: The Remaking of the Black American Ghetto." In *The Sociology of Norbert Elias,* edited by Steven Loyal and Stephen Quilley, 95–121. Cambridge: Cambridge University Press, 2005.

———. "Three Pernicious Premises in the Study of the American Ghetto." *International Journal of Urban and Regional Research* 21, no. 2 (1997): 341–53.

Wilson, James Q., and George L. Kelling. "Broken Windows: The Police and Neighborhood Safety." *Atlantic Magazine,* March 1982. http://www.theatlantic.com/magazine/archive/1982/03/broken-windows/4465.

Wolch, Jennifer. "From Global to Local: The Rise of Homelessness in Los Angeles during the 1980s." In *The City: Los Angeles and Urban Theory at the End of the 20th Century,* edited by Allen Scott and Edward Soja, 390–426. Berkeley: University of California Press, 1998.

Wright, Valerie. "The Expanding Federal Prison Population." Washington, DC:

Sentencing Project, 2011. http://sentencingproject.org/doc/publications/inc_
FederalPrisonFactsheet_March2011.pdf.

Yablonsky, Lewis. *Fathers and Sons: Life Stages in One of the Most Challenging of
All Family Relationships*. New York: Simon and Schuster, 1982.

Zilberg, Elana. *Space of Detention: The Making of a Transnational Gang Crisis
between Los Angeles and San Salvador*. Durham, NC: Duke University Press,
2011.

Index

Page numbers followed by the letter *f* indicate figures.